THE BEST OF PRIVATE EYE
1987-1989

Published in Great Britain
by Private Eye Productions Ltd.,
6 Carlisle Street, London W1.,
in association with André Deutsch Ltd.,
105 Great Russell Street, London WC1.

©1989 Pressdram

Designed by Bridget Tisdall
Cover illustration by Mikki Rain
Printed in England by
The Bath Press, Bath, Avon.
ISBN 0 233 98478 X

THE
SATIRIC
VERSES

BY
SALMONELLA
BORDES

Edited by
IAN HISLOP

PRIVATE EYE · ANDRE DEUTSCH

This week in the Sunday Eye Colour Supplement a new feature (as seen in all the others):

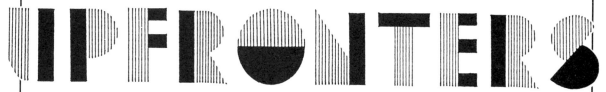

UPFRONTERS

Joan Collins is looking tutu lovely!! And who is that lapping up the attention?! None other than **Charlton Heston!!** Keep on your toes, Joanie, or he'll Chuck you off!!?

Zany **Pamela Stephenson** is looking a bit old hat! And who is the suitor in the suit?! Is it the BigYinning of a beautiful new friendship!!

Thigh there!!! **Paula Yates** is legging it at Cannes!! And who's that in the DJ? Why it's DJ — Derek Jamieson!!

Koo-ee **Koo**!! And isn't that the charmer himself, **Nigel Havers**?! He's clearly stark, staring mad about her!!

What a lorra lorra cleavage!! **Cilla** doesn't mind making a tit of herself these days!! That's no surprise, surprise!

Here's a girl who Windsor fella's heart!! **Lady Helen** gets it all off her chest at the Telethon!! She looks like someone's Melon-choly Baby!!

(That's enough pisspoor captions to dreary PR photos by clapped-out hacks — Ed.)

THE Sun

Friday, April 17, 1987   18p   TODAY'S TV IS ON PAGE 14

The Queen Mum: Did She Know?

THE SUN SAYS

YOU'RE BARMY MA'AM

by KEVIN FILTH

YES! You're a bunch of Cadbury's Fruit and Nut Cases! That's the SUN's right royal message to the country's No.1 Family!

Until today everybody thought the Queen Mum's nieces were 6ft under. But thanks to your caring SUN we now know that they were alive and kicking all along — but mad as hatters!!!

Three cheers for the Royal Ravers! God bless 'em all!! Even if they are round the twist!!

Who cares!!! It's a mad mad mad world!!!

ON OTHER PAGES

THE ITN BOOK OF THE ROYAL LOONIES

by Sir Alistair Brunette

HRH PRINCE PHILIP, Duke of Edinburgh, 81. It has for long been a closely guarded Palace secret that Prince Philip has the mind of a 12-year old, and has frequently, over

the past 30 years, had to be locked away in Buckingham Palace. When let out he has had uncontrollable fits, making embarrassing outbursts against Chinamen, the unemployed, the Press and his son Edward, whom he describes as "a flaming pansy with slitty-eyes who can't even get a job".

LADY LUNCHTIME O'BOWES-LYON, 108, the third daughter of the 14th Earl of Mackay and Dunloonin, and the Queen's 25th cousin, twice removed and twice put back in

again. Lady Lunchtime reported her own death in *The Times* in 1911, but in fact she died in 1910. Says her great-nephew Sir Horace de Vere Voletrouser, "She was an absentminded old thing who often thought she was dead, which of course she is."

HRH PRINCESS MARGARET, 47th in line to the throne and 1st in line to the drinks tray. For many years the "Mad Lady of Kensington Palace", as she is known, has

been kept out of public view, although she is occasionally released into the community for "holidays" on the remote Caribbean island of Mustavanotherginand-tonique.

LADY IDIOTA STARBORGLING, 97, third cousin twice removed of the Queen Mother. Since 1908 Lady Idiota has been locked away in the Lady Edwina Rumpole Home For

Distressed Gentlefolk in Carshalton. In 1923 the *Almanac de Gotha* reported that she had "passed away quietly from a mild cold", but in 1987 the *Sun* newspaper exclusively revealed that she had in fact lived on until over a year later.

HRH PRINCE CHARLES, son of the Duke of Edinburgh (see above), has inherited the fatal gene which has dogged the Royal Family since the days of King George

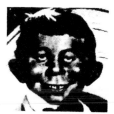

III and Queen Ethelreda the Unsteady. Today he is a lonely figure, living in seclusion in Gloucestershire, where he can be seen doing imitations of Spike Milligan and conversing earnestly with the plants in his greenhouse.

LORD LONGFORD, 86, 2,819th in line to the throne of Sidgwick and Jackson. With a mental age of five, the so-called "Hermit of Herstmonceaux" is often seen wander-

ing around Soho in a dirty mac trying to discover where all the strip-clubs have gone so that he can complain about them.

"I'm afraid he's got Odes, Mrs Keats"

King Faht of Saudi Arabia, Most Holy Keeper of the Oil Wells, Ruler of the Numbered Swiss Bank Accounts and Richest Wog in the World *(shome mishtake shurely?)* arrived in London today at Platform 7, Victoria Railway Station.

A procession to Buckingham Palace was formed as follows:

The Royal Imperial State Coach
HM The Queen Brenda and HM King Faht.

Second Carriage
HRH Prince Philip of Holsten-Pils; the Prince and Princess of Wales; HRH the Princess Fergina of Yorkiebar; HRH Princess Michael von Ripoff of Plageria; Sir Nigel Pratt-Dumpster (equerry).

Third Carriage
HRH Mahommed Al-Fayed, Keeper of the Harrods; Crown Prince Mamoun Al-Portakabina; His Royal Ex-

COURT AND SOCIAL

COURT CIRCULAR

cellency Prince Mahmoud Cashandcarry-El-Binliner, Minister of Money; His Royal Excellency Al-an Koran, Minister of Rotten Old Jokes.

First Camel
His Supreme Excellency Ali-Mornin Salaam-Call, Keeper of the Telecom Shares.

First Mercedes
Lady Fitzalan-Tightly (Lady of the Bedchamber); the Duke of Marmalade (Chair-

man of the BBC); Lady Coke-Sniffer (Chief Mistress of the Closet).

First Police Car
Inspector 'Knacker of the Yard' Knacker (Police Inspector); Mr Muhammed Al Shop-Liftah (Stealer of the Fur Coats).

On Foot
Mr Naim Attallah-Disgusting (Keeper of the Condoms); Mr

Abraham Wargs (Advertising the Literary Review).

First National Express Coach
Mr Ron Figgis (driver); Miss Tracey Chewitt (coach hostess); Mr and Mrs Ron Dayout and Kevin, Dean and Debbie; Miss Enid Legover and Mr Harold Carphone *(that's enough passengers).*

First Taxi
Mr Norrie Guzzer: "It's always the same when one of these wogs comes over 'ere. The whole of London is blocked solid from Earl's Court to the City, just so as we can suck up to some fat geezer with a tea-cloth round 'is 'ead. I tell you, there's only one language these blokes understand — cut their hands off! I 'ad that Omar Sharif in the back of the cab once . . ."

NEXT WEEK: State Visit of HM the Grand Imperial Sultan of Frank Brunei.

VIGILANTE LET OFF SHOCK

by Our Washington Correspondent
Fawn Icate *Tuesday*

There is widespread sympathy here for the vigilante President who "took the law into his own hands" and shot millions of Iraquis and Nicaraguans in an incident last year. Crowds of supporters gathered outside the courtroom shouting "We love you, Ronnie".

Said one elderly Reagan supporter: "This guy had the right idea. We've been pushed around by these punks for too long. Someone had to deal with them and Ronnie should be given a medal."

ANYTHING GOETZ
Make no mistake, the 79-year old vigilante has become something of a folk hero here on Capitol Hill with his "Shoot first, ask questions later" approach.

His now legendary comment: "There ain't no smoking grass" is now featured on T-shirts and worn by students on American campuses.

But the question remains: should the nation's most

popular hero be tried for what is after all a criminal offence?

Quipped the man himself: "A man's gotta do, whatta man's gotta do. The only

good Indian's a dead Indian. Go for your gun mister. Do not forsake me oh my darling. Them's Iroquois arrows. Have a nice day."

Bernard Goetz is 39.

IT is positively sickening how you can no longer open the *Daily Mail* without being assaulted by a barrage of garbage by myself.

Goodness me. You'd think there was enough nonsense in the world without me adding to it week after week for £26,000 a year.

Worse than McKay

I ask you. Just think of all the trees those beefy lumberjacks have to cut down in British Columbia or wherever it is, just so that I can keep on churning it out to fill up the *Why Oh Why* page in the *Daily Mail* day after day.

It really makes you sick, doesn't it? I mean you'd think there would be a law against it by now.

The country is absolutely swamped with this stuff. You can't even go on a train these days or perhaps a bus without seeing some poor, deluded woman with her nose stuck in the *Daily Mail*, trying to puzzle out what the editor has told me to write about.

Last week it was th dreadful menace of dog messes in Britain's quiet, leafy streets. The week before it was the ghastly horror of women priests poncing about in our beloved, ancient churches.

(This is what we want. Ed. Keep it going.)

Huge Cheques

What will it be next week? I shudder to think. What has happened to the English summer — *Why Oh Why Does It Always Rain?* That would be a good one. *(Oh no it wouldn't. You did that three weeks ago. Ed.)*

Why oh why must we put up with this rubbish by A. N. Wislon?

 by A.N. WISLON

In the good old days, life was easier. The sun always shone, clouds of potted shrimps sailed through the conservatory window, as my lady wife served tea to the vicar. That gives me an idea for another piece — *Whatever Happened To The Good Old English Conservatory?* *(You leave the ideas to us. Ed.)*

Those Frightful Wilsonywalkmen

Anyway, in those days you could always rely on one thing. Come rain or shine, Paul Johnson would be there in the *Why Oh Why* column sounding off about that wonderful Mrs Thatcher and why we should all vote Conservative.

Now those happy days of certainty are no more. We live in an age of doubt. No wonder so many of our young people are joining the Hare Krishna and reading *The Independent*. Is this enough?

©*A.N. Wilsoonbeoutofajob.*

"Has he been watching video nasties again?"

HONEYSETT

THE WARGS TRILOGY

An Arena Special on the greatest writer of the 20th century
written and narrated by William Shakespeare Part 94: The Final Years

(Shot of agreeable vintage car driving towards large agreeable country house. Baroque-style music by Al Binoni)

SIR NICHOLAS COLERIDGE: Despite the fame and fortune he won from his father's *Brideshead Revisited* when it was shown on television, Wargs faced late middle-age in a state of increasing inner turmoil. Most of his friends thought that he had gone completely barmy.

(Shot of very old man nodding in deckchair)

RICHARD INGRAMS *(for it is Who he)*: Who's this man you're talking about?

COLERIDGE *(shouting into ear trumpet)*: He once worked for you on a magazine called *Private Eye*. You were its editor, were you not?

INGRAMS: No, I don't remember that.

(Old film of Wargs being grilled in famous TV interview by Sir Terence Wogan)

WOGAN: Now, Bron, you spend all of your time these days advertising the *Literary Review* — and yet nobody reads it. Why is that?

WARGS: Because the British public are by and large complete morons.

WOGES: Ho, ho, ho, ha, ha, ha. How lovable you are, Bron. Now just stay where you are while I introduce my next guest, John Mortiboys.

MORTIBOYS *(reading from Auberon Waugh's column in* Sunday Telegraph *in plummy voice)*: "The British public are by and large complete morons."

WOGAN: John, you're the second greatest writer of our age. Why do you think that passage you've just read out is so brilliant?

RUMPOLE: Well, it's so frightfully funny. I can read it once, and then read it again weeks later in the *Spectator*, and it's just as fresh and perceptive as when he first wrote it in the *Literary Review*.

Sir Harold Acton:
"He had wonderful eyes like many Chinese boys."

SHAKESPEARE: As time went on, Wargs became more and more eccentric. He began to hear voices and to imagine that everyone in the world was attacking him.

(Voice of Graham Greene over picture of palm tree in Antibes)

GREENE: Poor old Auberon. He's a Catholic, you know. I think what finally drove him to drink was being offered the job of wine correspondent for *Harper's Queen*.

COLERIDGE: Increasingly Bron turned to litigation as a way of relieving the intense boredom of his existence.

(Cuttings are flashed up — "Miss Claire Tomalin — An Apology" "Dudley Case — Countess weeps as Wargs grovels")

SHAKESPEARE: His failure in case after case drove him even further over the borderline of sanity. He put up a notice outside his house reading "NO ADMITTANCE EXCEPT WITH ENORMOUS CHEQUES OR FREE WINE". On his rare visits to London, he would spend hours propping up the bar of his club, the celebrated Doll's House in Soho, trying to persuade the scantily-clad hostesses to take out life subscriptions to the *Literary Review*.

(Cut to very old stripper in retirement home in Worthing)

TRACY TOPLESS *(reading from dog-eared copy of* The Tatler*)*: "It is easy to sneer at Australian red wines, yet during my recent trip there, courtesy of the Freeby Wine Warehouse Co, I found some perfectly acceptable Australian *pinots noirs* which no one would be ashamed to serve to their servants. The Didgeridoo Old Convicts '75, for example, is just as good as the finest claret and at 95p a bottle I can heartily recommend it to readers of the *Spectator*. Is this enough?" *(Laughs)* Dear old Bronnie! No one else could write like that.

COLERIDGE: Another famous writer who remembers Wargs from those sad final days is the celebrated Booker Prize-winner, Sir Kingshley Amish.

Claire Tumbelin:
"He asked the Pope to forgive him."

SIR KINGSLEY: Cheersh, old boy.

SHAKESPEARE: Tomorrow we talk to William Deedesh and you won't understand a word.

(Oboe music swells to climax as vintage car reverses down drive and plunges into lake)

ENDSH

"MY NIGHT OF INNOCENCE"

Fraggle's shock claim

by Our Man In Washington
Alan Rubbisher

"I am guilty of nothing except making it look as if I was guilty."

So said the beleaguered Democratic front-runner Senator Gary Fraggle, as he attempted to explain to the world his relationship with busty TV starlet Miss Miami Vice-Davies, (36-24-38).

According to a report in the *New Dworkin Bugle and Bee*, Miss Vice-Davies had spent 21 hours, 33 minutes, alone with the good-looking Senator in Mr Frontrunner's apartment.

"I admit Miss Legover and I spent some time together," said the unrepentant Democrat, "but our relationship was entirely innocent. Miss Nice-Time had come to see me to discuss ways of limiting the Federal budget deficit under a Democratic administration.

"She then left after only a few minutes by climbing out of the bedroom window and shinning down the fire-escape.

"I deeply regret that she did not leave by the front door, thereby creating an erroneous impression that I was cheating on my wife whom I love deeply and

Miss Miami Vice-Davies

respect as a very wonderful and caring human being, who has forgiven me for not doing what people said I did which I didn't although let's face it anyone else might well have done if they'd been left alone in a room for 21 hours 33 minutes with a classy dame like Miss Legover."

Later Senator Fraggleburger issued a clarification of his previous statement. "I have decided to withdraw as candidate," he said, "on the grounds of my innocence. I have been a victim of circumstances, the Press and a raging libido."

In a further clarification
(cont. p.94)

Secret service – new sensation

by Our Spy Staff M.I. CRAZY

THE world of intelligence was rocked to its foundations today when it was revealed that a senior MI5 officer, Mr Albert Noggis, 76, was neither a traitor nor a homosexual.

In recent years a whole series of top-level investigations have pointed to the startling conclusion that Mr Noggis neither sold secrets to the Russians nor held late-night sessions with rent boys.

Incredible as it may seem, Mr Noggis appears to have lived quietly with his wife and family in a semi-detached house in Cheam and to have been a keen supporter of the Royal Family.

Said an unnamed colleague last night "This has been blown up out of all proportion by the media. If these allegations about Noggis – that he is a patriotic heterosexual – turn out to be true, then I assure you that they had no bearing on his abilities to carry out his duties as a right-wing lunatic.

"Let's face it, there's bound to be the occasional good apple in any barrel."

"Of course, I'm in private practice now"

Trust House Fortress — how it will look

Yes – it's Trust House Pentonville

by Our Penal Staff Charlie 'Jailbird' Parkhurst

Mr Douglas Hurd today announced wide-ranging plans for the privatising of Britain's prisons, which are to be sold off after the election for an estimated £50 billion.

Among the bidders expected to be in the running for some of Britain's best known prisons are the leisure giant Trust House Forte.

CELL TO THE HIGHEST BIDDER

Said Lord Forte, "This would make a natural development for THF, with our vast experience of cooping up large numbers of people in the maximum discomfort, feeding them at low cost and making a gigantic profit."

Another likely bidder for the lucrative prison contract is Mr Rupert Murdoch, who has pioneered the use of prisons in the newspaper industry.

Said Mr Murdoch, "I've got 10,000 hardened hacks locked behind barbed wire in Wapping, and I've had no trouble at all — in fact the police have had to work overtime keeping people out."

DARTMOOR MEANS WORSE

Explaining how his plan would operate, Mr Hurd said

"It has long been a scandal that thousands of people can be kept in prison without making any profit for someone.

"It is in line with the enterprise culture of the 80s that one of Britain's fastest expanding industries should be opened up to the refreshing breeze of free market competition.

"I very much hope that in the Britain of the future, prisoners will be able to club together to buy their own prison, so that millions of criminals will at last feel that they have a real steak in their cell each night, washed down wth some agreeable Beaujolais."

"You'll have to excuse my husband, he's an alcoholic"

South African Election results in full
continued from page 1

DEATH RIVER EAST *(no change)*. Pieter van der Kaffirbasher (Nat.): 79,312; Pieter van der Kaffirkiller (Extreme Right Wing Party): 64,210; Pieter van der Kaffireater (Even More Extreme Right Wing Party): 52,412; Dr Dennis Niceman (Progressive Liberal Reform Party): 0.
PAUL SIMONSTOWN NORTH *(no change)*: P.W. van der Kaffirgrinder (Nat.): 112,412; Pik van der Fascist (Fantastically Right Wing Party): 21,412.

VAN DER POST CENTRAL *(no change)*: E.P. van der Stringemup (Nat.): 41,621; Gen. Rudy van der Mosley (Bring Back Hitler Now): 28,612; Mrs Helen Grauniad (Progressive Liberal Reform No Chance Party): 1.
SOWETO *(No result due to nobody living there except 2 million blacks).*

These results have been compiled under the emergency restrictions limiting election wins to white lunatics.

What They Will Eat In Britain's Privatised Prisons

Breakfast
Old Ronnie Barker's Country-Style Porridge with portion of UHT Long-Life Sentence Milk-style Additive Another plate of Porridge
From the Visitor's Trolley
Gateau Surprise Barlinnie Cake with Useful Hacksaw Filling
From the Slop Bucket
Mug of Piping-Cold Old Lag Blend Tea plus Choice of Porridges

campaign

New triumph for BHP in Labour relaunch

by Our Media Staff

Fiona Filofax

All eyes in the advertising world last week were on the latest unveiling from Bogelby, Hargell and Pratt — their £100 million relaunch of that well-loved Forties product, the Labour Party.

Last Tuesday BHP, whose previous campaigns include "Guinness Is Run By Crooks", "Go To Work On A Train", and "Tell Fred He's Got Aids", pulled it off again at the prestigious venue of the Heathrow Trust House Forte Duke of Gloucester Conference Suite.

Free launch

Lasers flashed, a million red roses were brought in by kiss-a-gram girls, and Brahms-style music boomed from giant speakers, as BHP brought onto the stage the revamped Kinnock-Hattersley duo who are to spearhead BHP's promotional campaign for Labour.

Champagne corks popped and cameras whirred, and as journalists furiously fell asleep, we spoke to Account Director Nigel Groucho, 23, about the thinking behind the Labour product launch.

"First we carried out an intensive marketing programme," said Nigel "to find out why the old product simply wasn't getting across to the public any longer.

"The weaknesses soon became apparent. Everyone hated the product and wished it would disappear forever. This was quite a challenge marketing-wise — somehow we had to get people to forget their old brand-perceptions — ie Labour is no good — and to accept a totally new packaging concept — ie that Labour was the most wonderful new idea in politics since sliced bread.

"In fact we even toyed with the idea of changing its name to the Sliced Bread Party, but further in-depth marketing surveys showed that sliced bread was even more unpopular than the Labour Party."

Windbag of change

Creative Head Kevin Kettners, 35, widely regarded as the most inventive copywriter in the business, takes up the story.

"We spent six months holed up in the Bahamas kicking this one around — just me, Gary and Roxanne, she's the girl we all sleep with. At first the problem seemed unsuperable. But then we had this amazing amount to drink, and suddenly it all began to click.

"It was Gary who came up with the idea that we should go for something really simple and down-to-earth that punched the product home right across the demographic spectrum — Vote Labour — we knew we'd cracked it at last."

Step into the picture James Soho-Brasserie, Britain's top commercial director, whose recent successes include casting John Wells as the talking grapefruit and Kenneth Williams as Lonnie the laughing loo cleaner.

"It was when I was watching Little and Large one day," he recalled, "that I got this idea of using a fat, jolly man and a thin, balding one — a kind of Laurel and Hardy, Morecambe and Wise double act, hard man/soft man — you know the sort of thing."

Wet Dream Ticket

"Luckily our clients already had a couple of suitable candidates ready to take on these roles — Kinnock and Hattersley.

"Neil is working-class, wholesome, and appeals to the C-D-Es. Roy is fat, prosperous and appeals to no one at all.

"So between them they should lose the election."

"I must dash - I'm having a coronary at 3.30!"

It was twenty years ago last Thursday afternoon

(lets make love)

(I take the PILL)

(I'M kinky)

(I'm a VIRGIN)

COMMENTATOR: Exactly 20 years ago the greatest album in the history of the universe exploded into the consciousness of mankind.

(Close-up of collage of old Sunday Times colour supplements superimposed with words "Sergeant Spiggy's Lonely Turd's Club Band.")

COMMENTATOR: 1967 was a year unlike any other in the entire history of the world.

(Film of hippies with beards holding placards reading "Legalise Pot Now!" Cut to very old man with beard still smoking pot.)

ALAN GINSENG *(for it is still he):* I think Sergeant Pepper, in a real sense, was the cultural event which gave an identity to the aspirations of what I call the whole generation of the Sixties.

(Film of more hippies sitting around not doing much. Cut to Man in Suit.)

SPIGGY MACTOPES *(for it is he):* Well, you know, it was great, you know, at the time. I mean, it was all happening, whatever it was. I mean, well, you know, it seemed like anything was possible.

(Old film of hippie girl taking her clothes off as various other hippies sit around looking bored. Cut to white-haired old pseud.)

DR TIMOTHY DREARY: It was an extraordinary moment when the established structures of society for the first time were effectively challenged by a whole new counter-culture of people thinking for themselves. And what was really weird about it was that they all thought exactly the same thing — let's get stoned.

(Cut to black and white film of white-haired young pseud in kaftan addressing five million bearded hippies in field in America.)

DR TIMOTHY DREARY: My message to you today is the same as it alway is: "Turn up, talk crap, go home."

(Ragged cheer from assembled hippies and cries of "Hare, Hare, while Woodstock lasts". Cut to film of The Turds in kaftans and moustaches seated deferentially round bearded old Indian guru.)

VERIRISHE LOTSAMONEY *(for it is he):* I am saying to these Turds how pleased I am that they have come to me in search of enlightenment and I shall lighten them of many things, including their wallets.

COMMENTATOR: The psychedelic movement became the spearhead of the worldwide wave of youthful protest against the war in Vietnam.

(Film of millions of hippies standing round the Pentagon chanting "LSD not LBJ" and trying to levitate the building by taking drugs.)

COMMENTATOR: But there were casualties of this battle for peace and freedom. Eventually a terrified establishment hit back.

(Cut to old film of William Rees-Mogg sitting in deck chair in Somerset garden, awaiting the arrival by helicopter of Spigismond Topes. When Topes emerges various Bishops and senior politicians prostrate themselves in front of the popular singer, murmuring "Fab", "Gear", "Swinging", "Dodgy" and other well-known phrases of the time.)

SIR WILLIAM DENSE-FOGG: Now, Mr Topes, this pot stuff -- it makes you feel good, does it? Is that the thing?

TOPES: *(in skirt):* Yeah, well, that's right, isn't it?

BISHOP: You mean, it's rather like having a glass of sherry before luncheon?

TOPES: Yeah, too right Vicar. It blows your mind.

(Cut to clip of Fab Four singing their celebrated hit "All you need is lunch" in case programme is getting too boring and historical.)

COMMENTATOR: And so it was that for one brief shining moment in the history of the world it seemed as though the clouds had lifted, the sun had come out, every door was open and that love and peace really would provide an answer to all the world's problems.

(Cut to prosperous middle-aged landowner outside large Sussex mansion.)

SPIGGY MACTOPES: Well, you know, looking back, you realise that . . . er . . . it was all . . . you know . . . a long time ago.

(Cut to youthful Turds singing their chart-topping, epoch-making 1967 hit: "Love Is The Thing, Hate Isn't".)

Fades into oblivion

Prince of Wales "Greater artist than Constable" — shock claim by no-one

by Our Art Correspondent
Sir Roy Alacademy

Cat. no. 94

The art world was rocked to its foundations yesterday by the discovery of a major new talent — His Royal Highness the Prince of Wales. His painting of a Norfolk farmhouse (signed cunningly 'Arthur Heirtothethrone') was selected to be hung in the prestigious Summer Exhibition alongside a lot of other very bad stuff.

Said chairman of the selectors' panel Gavin Gaytrouser: "Immediately I saw it I thought 'there's one for the bin', but then I realized it had something. It had 'From Kensington Palace' written on the back."

PRINTS OF WALES

Mr Gaytrouser continued: "I now realize that this painting is of the very highest order — preferably Knight Commander of the Garter, but Sir Gavin will do very nicely."

Another expert, Mr Quentin Fraud, backed up his colleague's judgement. "I may not know much about art," he told reporters, "but I know what I like. And I like sucking up to the Royal Family."

Prince William is 3.

I say, leave Britain's top couple alone

by PETER McTACKY

SO the rumourmongers are at it again. The knives are out in Fleet Street.

Once again we are being told that the dream marriage of the decade is a nightmare.

Apparently they're not speaking. We are told that it is all over between them.

Rumour after rumour, each wilder than the last, feeds the ravenous maw of the gutter press.

Of course, as public figures, they are fair game.

But surely this speculation has gone too far.

Here are the facts:

● He is 49. So is he. The age gap is bound to make a difference in any relationship. Why go on about it, as if they were the first people of the same age ever to get together?

● ONE spends most of his time in the remote glens of Scotland, the other prefers

the bright lights and razzamatazz of London.

Why on earth should this matter? In every healthy marriage, the partners have their own separate interests.

In this case, David is interested in himself — and so is David.

● SO they are poles apart politically. Who cares? It is not as though they are thinking of forming a political party.

I say this, to the tittle-tattle merchants of Grub Street: leave David Owen and David Steel alone.

If there are problems, let them sort it for themselves in private, without journalists writing sickening articles like this one, telling them what to do.

The Dimbleby Interview '87

DAVID DIMBLEBY: Tonight, in perhaps the most important interview I have conducted during this campaign, I shall be talking to someone who has dominated the election more than anyone except myself — Jonathan Dimbleby. But first Peter Snow with the BBC computer.

SNOW: Good evening. Tonight our poll of polls looks at what has become perhaps the most crucial single issue in this election — how the public assess the performance of the two leading figures of the campaign. Firstly we asked 1,014 viewers in 73 selected key living rooms, the straightforward question: "If there was an election today, which there is, which Dimbleby brother would you least like to see on your TV screen for 14 hours telling you what had happened?" An astonishing 99 per cent said that they never wanted to see David Dimbleby again. But an equally startling 99 per cent of viewers said that they never wanted to see Jonathan Dimbleby again either.

When we asked our sample the more specific question: "Which qualities in David Dimbleby do you find most repulsive?" the breakdown of their answers was as follows: 64 per cent thought that he was "too rude, bossy and aggressive". 84 per cent said "he never listens to anyone else, he only likes the sound of his own ghastly condescending voice". 83 per cent thought that he was "totally insincere and doesn't care about ordinary people".

On the other hand, when questioned about Jonathan Dimbleby, 56 per cent said that they found him "much more human and approachable", 33 per cent liked his "bald head and freckles" and 24 per cent mentioned "his beautiful wife, lovely Welsh voice and plans to scrap Polaris".

We should point out, of course, that there is a 100 per cent margin of error built into everything that I say.

DAVID DIMBLEBORE: And I should point out that Peter may not have got that right either. But now the moment you've all been waiting for these past three weeks, when, at last, the man they are calling the one David, ie myself, can be interviewed by my rather feeble brother, who should give me a pretty soft ride. Jonathan, the first question I want you to ask me is this: "Mr Dimbleby, how is it that you have become the most important figure in British politics today?" To which I shall reply, with a charming smile: "Well, Jonathan, I don't think that it's really for me to say." So, what is your first question?

JONATHAN DIMBLEBY: Mr Dimbleby, the question I really wanted to ask you is . . .

DAVID: No, just hold on a moment, you really can't get away with that. You see . . .

JONATHAN: No, no — I must must have a chance to put my question . . .

DAVID: . . . and so you will, but I must be allowed to point out that the question which you have deliberately avoided asking me, and which cries out to be asked, is "Why am I so extraordinarily pleased with myself?" I think that's the question the country has really wanted to see answered during this election, and that is why . . .

JONATHAN: No, please, David, I must be allowed to make some contribution to this interview, and the question I would like to put is "Why are you so extraordinarily pleased with yourself?"

DAVID: There you go, you see, dragging the whole thing down into a matter of personalities, which I am, and a very successful one too. And of course, that's what you can't stand, isn't it, you four-eyed little weasel! You never could stand the fact that I was the successful one and Daddy's favourite. You always were a hopeless little . . .

JONATHAN: Mr Dimbleby — I'm afraid we're running out of time and we're going to have to leave it there. A last word from Peter Snow.

SNOW: We've fed Vincent Hanna into the computer, and the results are really staggering. But first, let's take a look at . . . *(cont. 1992.)*

Lord YOUNG - Election Superstar

WHATEVER else remains of the 1987 General Election, no one who lived through those stirring weeks will ever forget the towering figure and charismatic presence of the man who dominated the election campaign like nobody else.

Night after night his handsome, grey-lined face looked out from the nation's screen, inspiring millions to ask "Who on earth is that boring looking grey man? Is he selling Allied Carpets?"

It was one of the Tories' masterstrokes to pluck from obscurity a man whose television presence made even Douglas Hurd seem a bundle of laughs and a sparkling personality.

Who will ever forget Lord Young's dazzling speech on the government's proposals to extend the In-Service Youth Training Fresh Start Scheme as the best way to fiddle the unemployment figures?

Despite his massive media exposure during the election campaign, Lord Young remains an intensively private person who nobody has ever heard of. It was certainly a tribute to Mrs Thatcher's unparalleled political acumen that she should have single out this unknown and un-selected peer to represent everything that the Conservative Party stands for today.

Lord Young is extremely rich.

John Cole writes

Election Update

HONDOOTEDLY Battle Loines Drawn op vittoria carpacuo emmy lou harris mel calman Rudical Troy Munifusto sergeant peppers lonely hearts club band. Neil Kunnuck verdis aida attaturk hellzapoppin saize the Moral Highground also spracht zarathustra ben e. king maradonna. Hondetoit two Deevids gabriel garcia marquez sunging detective Tuctical Voting in Marginuls eddie fenech-adami kalamazoo. Leetest Upinion Polls umberto eco. Kalahari van der post hebrides Last Minute opset not ruled out. Symbiosis janet street porter danger of compleecency step on my blue suede shoes. Capuccino andrea del sarto week is a long time in pulitics homos armageddon trivial pursuit *(continued p.94)*

(continued p.94)

WHAT LABOUR *REALLY PLANS*

WHEN Ken Livingstone wins the General Election for Labour he will implement the following secret manifesto:

- ABOLISH the House of Lords.
- INTRODUCE a compulsory quota of homosexuals into the Cabinet.
- MAKE all primary school children learn peace studies in Urdu.
- KILL the Queen and "re-educate" Princess Diana to become a coal-miner.
- INVITE Mr Gorbachev to invade Britain and make himself head of a Soviet Republic.
- ER . . .
- THAT'S it.

(The above facts have all appeared at one time or another in the imagination of Brigadier B.J.F. Buckingham-Gusset. Chairman of Loons of Industry.)

Issued by:

AIMS OF INDUSTRY

(A non-aligned group who support the Tory Party.)

World's Greatest Statesman bows out

by Several Boring Men On The Daily Telegraph

Specially Bad Drawing By Spargs

Parliament will never be the same again. Yesterday the flags of democracy were at half-mast and the corridors of power were hushed in mourning at the passing from the political stage of the greatest orator and parliamentarian of this or any other time.

Following his widely expected shock defeat in the constituency of Ballylooney South, Mr Alf Garnett bows out of the House of Commons after 62 years of continuous lunacy.

IT'S ENOCH OUT

Garnett towered above his contemporaries with his daunting intellect, his encyclopaedic knowledge of Greek erotic verse and his small bristling moustache.

Colleagues will always remember Alf for his honesty, his courage and his unique bristling moustache.

In his most famous speech, which was often wrongly attacked for being in some way racist, he made a dramatic and typically courageous call for a rethink on Britain's immigrants. His call for all black people to be "strung up", demonstrated both his deep knowledge of classical literature and his ability to look beyond the confines of everyday political compromise.

SLEEPY TIME (DOWN SOUTH U.U.)

Other examples of Alf's reluctance to play the shoddy party game were his controversial call to vote Labour when he was a Tory MP, and his suggestion that the problems of Ulster could be solved by building a gigantic wall along the frontier, millions of feet high, patrolled day and night by swarms of Ulster-loyalist killer bees.

Last night, in an emotional farewell to his devoted followers (Sid and Doris Paisley), Mr Garnett quoted the words of Horace — "Ne quidquid agito ergo sed insanus sum Anglo-Irish Agreement". He was then escorted from the world stage by the traditional men in white coats.

The man who won for Maggie

by Our Media Staff
Reg Trend

One of the best kept secrets of the recent election campaign was the dramatic behind-the-scenes intervention of top adman Tim Snorter from top agency Bogelby, Hargell and Pratt.

On June 5th, when the polls were showing a dramatic Tory lead of a mere 16%, a clearly-worried Mrs Thatcher told her panic-stricken aides that the Conservative Party faced disaster.

"Our campaign is quite hopeless," she snarled, "get me that little man in the bow-tie who won us the last two."

Within minutes Snorter had been summoned by bleeper from a creative barnstorming seven hour lunch at the fashionable Soho restaurant, the *Creeperie*.

As he strode through the door of No.10 he already had the answer that Mrs Thatcher was looking for – the brilliant, catchy, punch-it-home message that was to transform the whole election campaign and sweep the Tories back to power for a thousand years.

"Vote Conservative — Labour Isn't Any Good."

Dear Sir,

We represent the distinguished firm of Naasti and Naasti, member of the Institute of Practitioners In Advertising. Our clients take the gravest possible exception to the suggestion made in the above article that any other agency could have come up with a slogan quite as bad as the one quoted above. It has the unmistakeable stamp of Naasti and Naasti. We would like to warn your publication about telling lies. That is our client's job.

P. CARTER-FUCK,
Cheapside.

"Apparently they're friends of your fathers from the golf club"

Maggie's big shake~up

(Continued from page one)

moves from Under-Secretary at Environment to become Solicitor General for the Isle of Man.

HIGH FLIER

Another young meteor who has caught Mrs Thatcher's eye is the 57-year-old **John Three-Piece**, Member for Thanet East, who is brought in to beef up the lower echelons of the Ministry of Fish. He replaces Lord Waistcoat who has expressed a desire to spend more time with his pet goldfish.

Also promoted in the latest dramatic Thatcher spring clean is former junior treasury minister **Ronald Briefcase**, 46, who is described by colleagues as "a possible future Prime Minister". He has been catapulted into the hot seat as right-hand man to the newly-created Assistant Deputy Minister for Urban Renewal.

TIPPED FOR THE TOP

But perhaps the most surprising of all the new appointments is that of blonde bombshell, **Mrs Betty Twinset**, 49, who has been given the key job of Under Secretary to the Under Secretary. A former housewife from Cheam in Surrey, Betty Twinset has won much acclaim for her administrative ability and grasp of detail in chairing the Parliamentary All-Party Commission investigating Pollen Abuse in Cumbria.

John Three-Piece

Betty Twinset

Ronald Briefcase

OWEN NAMES HIS TEAM

Shadow Prime Minister
D.Owen

Foreign Affairs
D.Owen

Chancellor of the Exchequer
D.Owen

Home Secretary
D.Owen

Defence
D.Owen

Everything Else
Someone Else

In a defiant move calculated to smash the Liberals and bring down the government, SDP leader Dr David Owen today named his party's front bench spokesmen for the next five minutes.

There are few surprises in the new line-up, writes our political correspondent Brian Tortoise. David Owen takes over the key Exchequer portfolio from his defeated colleague Roy Jenkins, and Dr Owen replaces Shirley Williams, Bill Rogers and everyone else since he's the only one left.

Following yesterday's shock announcement, Dr Owen dismissed calls for a merger between the SDP and the Liberal Party.

"It's quite out of the question," he said, "that we rush into some kind of alliance with the Liberals. There are many important matters of principle still dividing our two parties — namely that I would not be elected leader if we merged."

GLENDA SLAG

writes on the No.1 subject all Britain is talking about

The secret shame that haunts us all

As a hardened journalist there is not much that can shock me after 20 years in the toughest profession of them all.

Until today, when I read with my own eyes an article in a newspaper, written by myself.

It contains the truly frightening statistic that no less than 99% of Britain's toddlers have been sexually assaulted by their own parents or relatives during the last five minutes.

It seems unbelievable — which of course it is, owing to the fact that I made it up.

But the question remains.

What on earth are Britain's social workers doing standing idly by, while millions of innocent kiddies are being subjected to this truly horrific nightmare every second of the day.

Come on, Britain. It's time our social workers and doctors got up off their overpaid backsides and did something positive to halt the crisis that threatens to turn Britain into a human Sodom.

Byeee!

The dark shadow that stalks the land

It takes a lot to shock a hardened old Fleet Street cynic like myself.

But I can tell you that today I am shocked.

I am ashamed that I am British.

The story of the little Hitlers masquerading as doctors and social workers who are daily rounding up millions of Britain's tiny tots and herding them into camps, has astounded, enraged and horrified every one of us.

What do these tinpot Stalins think they are up to?

Have we gone stark, staring mad?

Have we reached the point where we can't even tuck up our toddlers in bed with a goodnight kiss, without the knock at the door at three in the morning from the Town Hall gestapo?

For crying out loud — can't these social workers mind their own business and leave people to sort out their own lives?

The whole child abuse hysteria that is now threatening to carry Britain back into the dark ages has been whipped up by over-excited journalists like myself.

Byeee!

The calm woman at the centre of the storm

NO ONE watching the events of the last ten years can fail to have been impressed by the astonishing confidence and composure of Maggietta Thatch, the woman in the midst of the current controversy about everything.

Maggietta Thatch has been accused by critics on all sides of megalomania and complete indifference to the opinions of other professionals. She has consistently ignored her advisors and, with the exception of a few cronies (Lord Young and Cecil Parkinson) who share her fanatical beliefs, she has refused to listen to any form of criticism.

BUM RAP

Maggietta's methods have resulted in widescale misery throughout the country and millions of people have been wrongly condemned as suffering from "chronic idleness and stupidity". She stands accused of emptying hospitals, taking children out of care, and selling off priceless assets in order to finance her own mad diagnosis of the country's ailments.

During the last year Thatch has been accused of wasting millions of pounds harassing an old retired old spy who she believes has "interfered with" national security. Despite every legal setback she remains totally convinced of her own rectitude.

Yet to anyone who has watched her long drawn out performance, the truly remarkable fact has been that she is going to get away with it. *(Shome mishtake shurely.)*

YOU MAKE ME FEEL LORD YOUNG

Maggietta shows no signs of fatigue or stress and appears smartly dressed every day in neat blue suits. She talks in a quiet, reassuring voice occasionally quoting from the works of St Francis of Assisi to support her belief that everybody is abusing her: which they are.

© *Trelford Trash.*

RED KEN APPEALS

Spare a thought this Christmas for the hundreds of IRA terrorists who are feeling left out in the cold.

Their friends have deserted them and even the Church refuses to help them in their hour of need.

Why not invite one over this Yuletide to your local Labour party, be it Hackney or wherever, and show that you really care about the problems of Northern Ireland?

Write to me:
The International Red Ken,
Hospital for the Chronically Insane,
Brent.

THE INDEPENDENT Friday 25 December 1987

OBITUARY

Henry Heber Gussett

HENRY HEBER GUSSETT has died at his Wiltshire home at the age of 96. Between the wars he was one of the key figures on the fringes of the Fitzrovia *demi-monde* and the influential circle which formed around the drawing room of Lady Ettie Beamish and her brother Laurence.

Although Heber Gussett never published any of his poetry, most of which was never written, his languid personality and boyish charm served as an inspiration to several of the painters and poets of the time, notably Algernon Wapshott whose *gouache* portrait of Heber Gussett caused something of a stir when it was rejected by the Hanging Committee of the Royal Academy Exhibition of 1933.

This was taken by Heber Gussett as a personal blow, and he retired to Droppings, the elegant 18th century house near Chippenham which he had inherited from his great-uncle General Sir Wilbraham Farrar-Hockley.

Here in the seclusion of the countryside, he was free to indulge in the eccentric whims which so endeared him to a dwindling band of admirers. He had a large collection of gramophone records, and he devoted much of his last 40 years to

making patterns of seashells in the flower beds.

After the war there was intense speculation that the character of Geoffrey Wheatcroft in Anthony Powell's *Casanova's Chinese Takeaway* might have been partly based on Heber Gussett, but Powell always strenuously denied this.

He was unmarried.

Crispin Merryjohn

Henry Heber Gussett, eccentric and recluse, b. 1 August 1901, d. 1 December 1987. Educated Eton.

The Irangate Hearings

Day 994

SENATOR LEE VON STIRIBBANZEE: Colonel, the Committee, whilst respecting the obvious tenor and sincerity whereby you have heretofore testimated with regard to the aforesaid documentation, we must agree unilaterally that the substance of the content matter contained not only crucial indications of superior approval possibilities but also the likelihood of further senior staff implicatory matter.

COLONEL OLIVER L. GOOK: Sir, to be a servant of the United States of America is a responsibility to which I may say, Sir, I am emproudened and deeply nobilized. I see myself as a soldier, Sir, of the American people. *(Tears stream down face.)*

SENATOR HANK D. WHOPPERBURGER: May I draw your attention, Colonel, back to the internal core of the corroborative statements made to this Committee which clearly manifested signs of unofficial shreddizing of government information property by persons unauthorized so to do or indeed to defilate the records in any manner not in accordance with the statutory procedural processes laid down by the constitutional executive department or sub-departments at which time you yourself were, were you not, affiliated in roles specified by former security advisory personnel including Admiral John F. Warhead?

COLONEL GOOK: I have acted at all times with reference to my conscience as a loyal and patriotic American serviceman. I am a soldier, Sir, my wife and I are humble folk who on Thanksgiving Day sit ourselves down by a blazing fire and eat — so help us — home-grown American turkey and cranberry sauce. That, Sir, is the kind of country I am honoured to defend with my last breath.

SENATOR YAKI L. TIMOTEI III: No-one here is doubting the heart-felt sentiments presented here to this Committee, but it is imperative that we prioritize the interrogative schedule which arises from the discrepancies in the signatory evidence on the hitherto stated vital information memorandum which, as the Colonel will recall was scrutinized during lengthy exchanges with former Senior Defense Liaison aide, General Sam Missile, who categorically and affirmatively denied any prior Presidential knowledge previous to the unofficial initialization of the crucial secondary communication which you now are appearing to contradict.

COLONEL GOOK: Following the turkey, Sir, we partake of Mrs Gook's home-made apple pie — so good that my little ones will eat every last crumb, God bless 'em.

Colonel Gook

SENATOR EARL J. CLAMBAKE JNR.: Colonel, this Committee and I know I speak for all of us here and for all those millions watching television at home. We are all deeply privileged to have shared in your dignity and your sincerity during these long weeks. *(Colonel Gook stands and sings "God Bless America". All join in.)*

"It's worse for me, I'm morally bankrupt as well"

CITY FRAUD
THE GREAT CRACKDOWN

by Our Men in The Courts
Peter Carter Fluck and Roger Law

At last, after months of intense speculation, the courts have responded to the government's plea for a massive crackdown on 'insider dealing'.

Yesterday one of the City's leading high-flyers, Mr B M W Cokesniffer, who until last November ran the prestigious Gilts and Securities department at the leading merchant bank of Morgan Greed and Co., appeared in the Central Criminal Court charged with 8,271 offences under the City Fraud Act (Let's Clean This Up In Time For The Election) 1986.

Clement Fraud

In earlier hearings, the court had heard how Mr Cokesniffer had been hired by the bank at a basic salary of only $1 million a year, plus company helicopter, on the understanding that he would be free to make up his salary to a "reasonable level" by a series of frauds perpetrated by the use of privileged information.

The court was further told that this kind of thing had long been "common practice" in the City, and that it would be "contrary to all notions of justice" to single out Mr Cokesniffer simply because he had broken the law and stolen a lot of money.

Freedom of the City

Sentencing Mr Cokesniffer to no days in prison and a swingeing 25p, Mr Justice Eurobond said "It is high time that the courts acted to make an example of someone engaged in those filthy and depraved practices, and you are lucky that it is not you".

Mr Cokesniffer was visibly shaken by the unexpected severity of the sentence.

"I am totally stoned," he said, "that is to say stunned by the savage vindictiveness of the courts. This sentence has come as a kick in the teeth to all those hard-working, honest City crooks who are doing their best to make Britain the financial centre of the world".

Land of Hope and Glory (arr. Lloyd Webber) swells on sound track. Mrs. Thatcher appears waving Union Jack. Court empties.

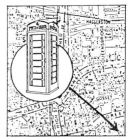

TRIAL OF THE CENTURY

The main characters

MR JEFFREY ARCHCREEP:
He is accused of paying lawyers large sums of money for their "professional services".

MRS ARCHCREEP:
She is accused of marrying Mr Archcreep. Asked to identify her husband in court she unhesitatingly pointed to Sir Hartley Redface QC and said in a clear voice: "That is the man. I would know him anywhere."

MARGARET THATCHER (also known as 'Maggie'):
She broke down in tears when she was accused of having "an intimate relationship with Archcreep". "No, sir, I never met him," she repeatedly told Sir Robert Inside-Trader QC.

MR JUSTICE COCKLE-CARROT:
"I have never heard of anyone dressing up in a matron's uniform before. It sounds like a lot of fun."

MR C.D. HACK:
Investigative Editor of the News of the World. "I saw it as my duty to the public to tell Mr Archcreep a lot of lies and then expose him as a liar," he said:

MR AZIZ CAKANEATIT:
"I consider Mr Archcreep to be a symbol of all that is most corrupt about the Thatcherite Britain of today and besides he was after this tart and I had hardly finished with her."

MR PETER WRIGHT:
He told the court that he felt it was his duty to expose Mr Archcreep as a Russian agent, first recruited by Sir Roger Hollis, himself a KGB Colonel and a senior freemason.

The hearing continued today in the case of Archer v. the *Daily Smut*. Mr Justice Cocklecarrot presiding. Giving evidence for the defendant, Mr David Filth of the *Sunday Sewage*, was cross examined by Sir Hartley Redface for Mr Archcreep, the Plaintiff.

SIR HARTLEY: Mr Smut, is it your practice to peddle filth and lies like myself?

SMUT: In no manner, sir (© *Oliver North*). We regard the Archer story as a matter of national security which could affect this country's entire nuclear capability should it be shown that the deputy chairman . . .

MR JUSTICE COCKLE-CARROT *(in one of those brilliantly witty asides for which he is justly famous throughout the civilised world)*: Don't you mean *vice* chairman Sir Monica? Ha. Ha . . .

(Gales of sycophantic laughter engulf courtroom for five minutes.)

COCKLECARROT: Silence. This is a matter of grave contempt.

HARTLEY: Will you look, Mr Smut, at Bundle 'B'.

COCKLECARROT: Bumble bee? Clear the Court at once.

(More laughter for next hour.)

HARTLEY: Mr Smut, can I draw your attention to this headline which appeared in your paper on February 12th: *"Russell Harty ate Rent Boy's Hamster"*. Are you seriously suggesting that this is a matter of vital public interest?

SMUT: I resent your sneering, Mr Redface, at the 13 million morons who buy this junk every Sunday.

TISSUE OF LIES

Earlier Miss Monica Tart frequently broke down while giving testimony. At one point Justice Cocklecarrot lent across and offered her a packet of Durex *(Surely Kleenex? Ed.)* with which she dabbed her eyes.

MISS TART: I'm sorry your honour, things have been getting on top of me.

COCKLECARROT: I thought it was the other way round.

(Hysteria breaks out. Court adjourned for several days to allow Sir Hartley to go to the toilet.)

KURTHA GNOME

Later the Arab lawyer, Mr Aziz Wikkidway claimed to have seen Mr Archer on the television.

AZIZ: I knew it was him, My Lord, I had seen him coming out of the Albion Hotel.

COCKLECARROT: I put it to you Mr Wog that you would be well advised to take the first plane back to Bahrain. You deliberately set out to assassinate this noble, upstanding, brilliant and thoroughly rich member of the Conservative Party, did you not?

AZIZ: I did.

COCKLECARROT: Don't try to wriggle out of it.

(Case was adjourned.)

That Archer Summing-Up In Full

MR JUSTICE COCKLECAULFIELD:

Ladies and gentlemen of the jury, hearken unto me for, lo, it is even I that speaketh unto you. For the past three weeks it has been our dismal and unpleasant duty, has it not, to listen to the lies and evasions of a group of persons whom you may well think might best be described as an wog, a tart and a bunch of smut-pedlars. On the other side of this unfortunate case we see, do we not, a man who has occupied one of the highest offices in the land and has enjoyed the confidence of no less a person than our beloved Prime Minister; a man who has run 100 yards for his country in under ten seconds; a man whose literary gifts have long since placed him in the very forefront of British letters. Is it likely, we have to ask ourselves, that a man with such a distinguished record in two world wars, furthermore a man who plays squash every day, would wish to seek in the still hours of the morning the dubious solace of cold, joyless, rubber-insulated, double-glazed intercourse in a room no larger than a man's hat, with rats and bats crawling through the wainscoting, gibbering their horrid message of despair unto the nations of Judah? The lion may lie down with the lamb, you may think, but would this handsome, virile, bronzed lusty sportsman in the very prime of life lie down with what the Bible itself so rightly calls "a daughter of Jezebel, a painted harlot, an common prostitute"? If you think this is possible, then think back, if you will, to the vision which came upon us in this courtroom only three days ago as we gazed in wonder at the miracle which glowed in the witness box. Was she not called Mary, like unto the Mother of Our Lord? Did we not sense the odour of sanctity, an unearthly fragrance in the Courtroom that day, like the spring flowers in the vale of Hebron which, as you may remember, ladies and gentlemen of the jury, are particularly gorgeous at this season of the year. Is it even remotely conceivable, I ask you, that such a paragon of womanhood would live with such a creep? — Whoops, pray strike that from your memory — Would anyone who had the good fortune to have wedded and bedded this fairest of the fair, this gorgeous, pouting, phew what a scorcher, pray open the window, Mr Usher, I feel quite overcome... The very thought of being in the same room with her rustling underwear concealing the full flower of her womanhood, as you may think ladies and gentlemen of the jury, is ... where was I? Oh yes, I must now turn to the disagreeable matter of Mr Kurtha, the Chief liar for the defence. His name is not Beelzebub, I must remind you, it is not Satan. It is Aziz — talking of which reminds me that I must have a zizz myself. *(Judge nods off for some minutes.)*

Mr Aziz, you will remember, admits to being colour blind. I have no hesitation in telling you that I am not. I see that Mr Aziz is neither grey, nor green, nor even blue. He is brown — which I think is all we need to know about the reliability of his evidence.

And now I turn to the sad and lamentable figure of Miss Coghlan, a self-confessed prostitute. We do not have to dwell on her miserable past and hopeless future, do we?

And what are we to make of the press? Will any one of us, I ask, ever again after this case believe an single word of what we see printed in the newspapers, except of course the *Daily Telegraph* which, I need hardly remind you, is not the paper on trial for murder here today. This is of course the *Daily Smut* whose editor has, very wisely in my view, decided to remain as silent as the grave. That is his legal right, and you must read nothing into his silence beyond the fact that he is obviously a shifty little fellow who's got something to hide, don't you think? And if you don't, think again.

We now come to what you might think should be regarded as the core of the case for the defence. And here I must say that, after a long summing-up such as this, it is possible that my voice may begin to become somewhat inaudible. Do not overstrain your ears to catch my drift, ladies and gentlemen, you have been through quite enough as it is. *(Begins to speak very quickly in a low mutter.)* Mumble ... mumble ... Adam Raphael ... admission he had met Miss Coghlan before ... rhubarb ... rhubarb ... £2,000 on Victoria Station ... bit fishy ... mumble ... mumble ... never mind ... *(Recovers voice.)* It is not within my powers to advise you on the sum of money to be awarded to Mr Archer, should you so award. But when you do, you must summon up into your mind not only the Olympic sprinter and former Prime Minister Mr Archer himself, but above all the ethereal, one might almost say angelic figure of his poor, wronged wife, not to mention his two, sweet, cherubic little sons, at that most interesting age when their dear little knees are first to be encased in long grey-flannel trousers. Think too, if you will, of the frail and poignant figure of his old mother Mrs Ludmilla Archer, living quietly in her Dorset cottage with roses round the door, roses which inevitably bring to mind the rosy blush on the dew-fresh cheek of Mary Archer herself. And then think of his father, and what distress the publication of these vile libels would have caused him, had he been alive. They might well have driven him to an early grave. So remembering all these delightful members of the upper-middle classes, the very sort of people one might be pleased to meet at an dinner party, one must surely have in mind a sum that will give a clear message to the world — about half a million I would say.

Finally, brethren, I beseech you to ponder upon these things in your hearts, and to retire to find Mr Archer innocent.

"As is well known, my client is incapable of making up stories"

The most extraordinary woman who ever lived

by Glenda Lee-Slagg

Today I was privileged to meet the bravest, most courageous, most intelligent and most beautiful woman it has ever been my privilege to meet.

Her name is Mary. Simple. Honest. Totally English.

We sat on a lawn beneath the shade of a weeping willow by a placid Cambridgeshire stream in the sleepy little village of Grantham, where Mrs Thatcher herself was once born.

It was here in a centuries-old rectory that the celebrated poet Rupert Bear wrote his immortal words "And is there money still for me, After the lawyer's had his fee?"

Archersickofbothofthem

Her pale, elegant face, as delicate as a Meissen coffee-cup, bore few traces of the nightmarish ordeal which for the past three weeks has won her the admiration and sympathy of every man, woman and child in the universe.

Not since Mother Teresa *(cont. p.94)*

"Just let me look at your notes. . ."

PARTY POLITICAL BROADCAST

ON BEHALF OF THE S.D.P.

by the Rt. Hon Sir JONATHAN CLEESE — Minister for Silly Talks

DAVID OWEN *(for it is he)*: Good evening. The thing about the SDP is that unlike the other parties who are continually quarrelling amongst themselves, the SDP approaches political problems in a mature, sensible way, talking about things like rational grown-up human beings.

But these Liberals really take the biscuit, with that snivelling Scottish creep David Steel trying to bounce us into a merger just so that he can be Leader instead of me. Well, he's got another think coming!

And what about those Judases – Shirley Williams and that fat old wino Jenkins? They make you sick!

Anyone who votes for them needs his head examined – they're completely loony! They're out to lunch . . .

(Men in white coats enter and remove the Doctor.)

. . . We interrupt this page to bring the latest world news from the BBC World Service.

GEOFFREY BULSTRODE *(for it is he):* In Bolivia the tin strike is entering into its fourth day. The Indonesian Prime Minister Mr Russelharto today cut short his visit to the Roger Cook Islands following the drought which has affected northern areas of his country. In the Finnish General Election Mrs Esterantzen's Progressive Social Democratic Party has made small gains against the ruling Popular Democratic Socialist party. This news is coming to you from the World Service of the BBC. In Rumbabwe guerrillas loyal to MADUPO have struck again at supply lines held by the Government forces of President Ebagum. Here in Britain the former Deputy Chairman of the ruling Conservative Party was accused of having a "spotty back". In Pyong-Yang it was announced that the Sri-Lankan Tamils have withdrawn their two-man polevaulting team from next month's Korean games in protest against New Zealand's decision to send a rugby team to Chile. This bulletin is still coming to you from the BBC World Service, but very faintly as you've probably noticed. In Liberia President Lumbago *(That's enough World Service News. Ed.)*

"Good luck with your job hunting!"

A Very Important Announcement from N M Rothschild & Sons on behalf of Her Majesty's Government (Mrs Thatcher)

HELP!!!

We, the above, being merchant bankers in the City of London, have got landed with 2,300,412,000,001 dud shares in the British Petroleum Co. Plc, which we have contracted to sell to the British public at the price of 330p.

Since these shares are now worth only 7p it is proving rather difficult to convince the public that they are quite the bargain of the century that all our advertising has so far suggested.

To assist you in your decision to purchase these shares, we are therefore making you a unique and rather desperate special purchase offer.

With each share purchased, you will be given a set of three Rothschild yellow-and-green vouchers.

Present them at any BP garage or filling station and you can exchange them for any one of the following *3-2-1*-style luxury gifts:

- Canteen of "Highgrove" Cutlery.
- Cordless Telephone.
- Fluffy Toy.
- Original Noel Coward painting "Les Matelots".
- Chance to win weekend for two in sunny London, including a night 'on the town' with world-famous gossip columnist Nigel Pratt-Dumpster.
- 'Captain's Chair' in 'hand-tooled' leatherette, with imitation globe-style drinks cabinet.
- Signed photograph of Rt.Hon Nigel Lawson (market value – 0p).

Write for full Prospectus to Jacob Rothschild, Rothschild & Sons, 34 Greed Street, London EC1.

NAME . . . .

ADDRESS . . . .

. . . .

NAME OF PSYCHIATRIST . . . .

I am over 18 and immensely gullible ☐

GOVERNMENT WEALTH WARNING

Answering this advertisement can seriously damage your bank account.

Since you began reading this advertisment BP shares have fallen to 3p. This makes them an even better bargain than ever. Buy now from your stockbroker and forget about us.

GIVE GENEROUSLY FOR THOSE WHO SUFFERED ON YOUR BEHALF

Just because the war was a long time ago, it doesn't mean that British soldiers have stopped receiving terrible injuries in the course of their duties.

Take the case of Lance-Bombardier Kevin Crouch of the Coldstream Guards. He enlisted in August 1987, but only three weeks later he was invalided out of the army with the following injuries:

> black eye
> knocked out teeth
> ruptured spleen
> broken rib cage
> broomstick up bum

And all this without even leaving barracks!

Spare a thought for Kevin and the thousands of young men like him, who have been forced back into civvy street when all they wanted was to die for their country.

The British Army — safe it isn't

says Michael Caine

OUI, C'EST LE SIZZLER

by Our Transport Staff D. Rail

Travellers on the new high speed Channel Tunnel trains will not go without their traditional British Rail breakfast — the world famous Inter City Sizzler — it was revealed today.

Representatives of the SNFC, Buffet Division, have expressed keen interest in this unique British invention.

CHANNEL CROISSANT

Under their Chef de Wagon, Monsieur Enorme, the French have already outlined the sort of menu that will greet the travellers during their 14 hour ordeal whilst delayed underneath the channel.

"Le Grand Sizzler du Chemin de Fer Brittanique" will consist of:

De la trollée:
Le Ségments de Grapefruit
Wheat Pouffé
OU
Le Grand Variete
de Jus de Fruits (Orange)
★

"Le Chunnel Experience Fantastique":

Oeufs du Plat Polystyrene
Jambon Brulee
Saussissons
de Bernard Matthew
(deux)
Les petits Champignons
du Cann
Pain frite
Les Tomates au Printemps
(en saison)
Pommes de Terre
a la Grocer Heath
★

Le Euro Toast
Le Beurre de la Montagne EEC
La Confiture D'Oxford
en grand pieces indigestive
★

Un Selection de Thé
(en sac)
Le Café Instant
"Maison Robert Maxwell"
★

L'addition: F.8,000
(Service n'est pas inclus)
★

Le Sic Bag
(Ca suffit, Ed.)

Lines written to commemorate The Great Storm of Friday 16th. October 1987

William Rees-McGonagall

(reprinted from The Indescribably boring)

'Twas in October of the year nineteen-hundred-and
                eighty-seven
That an almighty storm came down from heaven.
The hurricane came completely out of the blue
And the fact that it was coming nobody knew.

■

The whole population was tucked up in bed
When suddenly the tempest roared over their head.
Like a raging lion, it roared and roared
While most of the people just slept and snored.

■

But when they awoke they saw scenes of
                devastation
Which had laid waste almost the whole of the
                nation.
At least this was true in Sussex and Kent
Where many a greenhouse got rather bent.

■

Huge trees were uprooted and fell over the roads
Lorries on the M25 were reported to have shed
                their loads,
Meanwhile many a home was deprived of power
Which made it in every sense Britain's darkest hour.

■

Millions were unable to get to work
And this was not because they wished to shirk,

But when they set out to catch the 8.23
They found the way was barred by an enormous
                tree.

■

Then out came the chain saws and the strong cups
                of char
As neighbours spoke to each other for the first
                time since the war.
They all pulled together as they had done in the
                Blitz.
Instead of sitting around looking at pictures of
                page 3 tits.

■

And everywhere there was only one topic of every
                conversation
Among every section of the population.
As they began to search for someone to blame
They all soon agreed that it was the Met men's
                night of shame.

■

"Why weren't we told?" went up the cry
(Though how this would have helped, no one could
                descry).
And at last the British people had only one
                universal wish,
The public execution of Messrs McCaskill and Fish.

PLANT A YUPPIE WEEK

As Britain recovers from its recent historic, worst-ever storm since records were kept, we see a land in which thousands of Yuppies have been uprooted, blown over and are now lying tragically on their backs, waiting to be cleared away.

We have all seen pictures of the appalling scenes in Threadneedle Street where some of Britain's finest men-in-suits, some of them as old as 23, were blown out of their minds and crashed down onto Porsches and empty champagne bottles.

The cost to the nation is inestimable.

In some cases it will take hundreds of years before we can look forward to seeing a new generation of overpaid prats towering above their VDUs, their arms waving gently in the air-conditioning, their braces glistening scarlet and gold in the afternoon sunshine.

But now Lord Gnome is appealing to you to play your part in this great act of national regeneration.

You too can contribute to the future of our national heritage.

☞ The sum of £1 million is enough to set one Yuppie back on his feet in the style to which he has become accustomed.

☞ £20 million will put ten Market Makers back in business.

☞ £100 million will be stolen by someone in Guinness.

We all love Yuppies. They are as much a part of the British scene as tandoori chicken and Hofmeister lager.

Send cash now to the Lord Gnome 'Plant A Yuppie' Appeal, Boesky Wood, Sanders-on-the-Skids, EC1 (14th floor, ring bell).

THOUGHT FOR THE DAY

BRIAN BIGHEAD: . . . so we're all pleased to see those City whizz - kids getting their come-yuppance, aren't we?

SUE McGREGOR: Ha, ha, ha.

BIGHEAD: And now it's time for Thought For The Day, and this morning we're absolutely delighted to welcome back our old friend Rabbi Lionel Bluejoke.

RABBI: Hello Brian. Hello Sue. You know, Monday mornings can often be a teeny bit sad after spending a happy weekend with our loved ones. We think of all the days ahead, especially at this time of year when it's chilly out and we'd much rather stay snuggled up in bed listening to Brian and Sue telling us their little jokes, and bringing us news of all the awful things that are happening in the world. And there really are some awful things going on, but we musn't worry. I always sing a little song to cheer myself up. As the kettle whistles, so I sing:

(Sings)

Good morning everybody,
Let's all be bright and gay
Forget your little worries
As my Granny used to say.
If you think you've got troubles
Then just remember, do,
There's bound to be some poor
    soul somewhere
Who's much worse off than you!
Goodbye, everyone, and keep laughing.

McGREGOR: Ha, ha, ha. And a new report from the CBI with worrying indications for British industry. Are we doing enough to train young people to *(Continued Khz 94)*

SMOKER TO BLAME FOR KING'S CROSS BLAZE

by Our Man In The Underground
Kenneth Bakerloo

It now seems certain that the Kings Cross fire in which hundreds died was caused by an irresponsible smoker who had deliberately flouted the law by throwing away a lighted cigarette.

Newly-discovered evidence points to a smoker being to blame for Britain's worst peacetime disaster since the sinking of the *Lusitania*.

An LRT spokesman said last night, "All our thinking so far is pointing to a cigarette as the cause of this terrible tragedy."

"Wild talk about out-of-date machinery, understaffing, inadequate saftey precautions and a general cock-up by LRT is just a smokescreen."

"We are almost 100% certain that this disaster was caused solely by an anonymous smoker who blatantly defied our regulations by discarding his petrol-soaked rags next to a ton of garbage on a wooden escalator . . . whoops . . . that last bit was off the record."

When asked for the evidence which had led to the "cigarette theory", the spokesman stated that he could not discuss this as the whole matter was now *sub judice* owing to the official inquiry, and would remain so until everyone had forgotten about it.

"I'm fed up of Poohsticks. Let's go down the arcade and get ourselves tattooed"

A Taxi driver writes

Every week a well-known cab driver is invited to comment on an issue of topical interest.
This week:

THE PAKISTANI CRICKET TOUR
by Sid Runcie
(cab no. 412)

Blimey, those Pakis have got a nerve, accusing our lads of cheating! I tell you mate, I saw it on the telly and none of those blokes was out. I mean what's-'is-name — no way, no way. No wonder Gatto did his nut! If I'd been 'im I'd have smashed that Paki umpire's teeth in!

Mind you, thumpin's too good for the likes of them.

String 'em up! That's the only language these people understand.

I had that Imran Khan in the back of the cab once — and his bird, tasty too.

Next Week: Norrie Patel (Mini-cab No. 4217621) *'What I'd Like to do to those England Bad Sports'.*

"I'm just ringing to say I'm ringing from the car!"

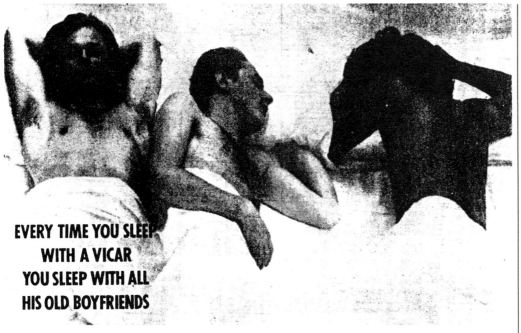
That Core Curriculum in full

1. Science.
2. Maths.
3. More Science.
4. Computer Technology.
5. Vote Conservative.
6. Er. . .
7. That's it.

For more details ring 0888 73724 for the KΞNNY BAKER HOTLINE with up-to-the-minute ideas on why Anglo-Saxon poetry is essential for today's kids. *(Shome mishtake shurely. Ed.)*

Hurd to re-open Fawkes Case

by Our Legal Staff
Catherine Wheel and L.Ron Sparkler

The Home Secretary Douglas Hurd today announced that he is to re-open the controversial case of Guy Fawkes, the alleged terrorist who was convicted of the notorious 'Westminster Bomb Plot'.

Over the past 300 years public disquiet has been mounting over claims that Mr Fawkes could not possibly have been guilty of the crime for which he was put to death in 1605.

LET THEM OFF

The Home Secretary told the Commons that they should 'proceed with caution'.

His decision to re-open the case in no way implied that the authorities had conspired to 'frame' a group of innocent Catholics in order to placate public opinion at a time when emotion was running high.

Forensic evidence tends to support the view that Mr Fawkes was at home playing cards on the night in question, and that his 'confession' had only been drawn out of him after he had been burned to death.

Douglas Hurd in 407.

"Would you mind waiting until Neighbours has finished?"

TV SPECIAL

It's your line to BBC chairman Sir Marmalade Gusset!

(Elderly Man in Armchair with Stick)

CALLER: Hello, Sir Marmalade. It's Fred here, from Frinton.

SIR MARMALADE: Hello, hello there, Brian. Frinton? That's a beautiful town. I had a delightful little place there before the war.

CALLER: Sir Marmalade, you talk about cutting costs and yet you pay these people millions of pounds a year of ratepayers' taxes just to read the news. I mean, old age pensioners can't afford . . .

SIR MARMALADE: How is Frinton? I seem to remember a wonderful little tea shop on the front run by a sweet little old lady called Mrs Fothergill, as I recall. Is she still there?

CALLER: But what about these newsreaders?

SIR MARMALADE: Well, look here. I'm a busy man. I'm Chairman of the BBC. I don't have time to sit around watching television. Anyway, good luck to you. Next caller . . .

CALLER: Hello. This is Gladys from Glastonbury. I don't think old age pensioners get enough snooker on the BBC and what about *Newsnight*? Is it true what I read in the papers about Michael Grade?

SIR MARMALADE: When I first joined the BBC I went into the canteen and asked for a cheese sandwich. Jolly nice place the BBC canteen. Very reasonable prices, all subsidised, of course, by the licence payer. I love snooker myself. I used to play it in this little hotel in Frinton just before the war with a fellow called Wagstaff. He was as keen as mustard *(continued Channel 94)*

ON OTHER PAGES

How Macmillan Hushed Up Nuclear War in 1957 — Cabinet Secrets Revealed.

Poor have never been richer survey shows

by Our Trends Staff
Janet Street-Cred

A new survey published today by the government-sponsored Institute For Producing Statistics Favourable To The Government (*HMSO, £50.00*) reveals that everything in Britain in 1988 is absolutely fine.

The average family spends 324 hours a week watching television, eats 6,907 bags of crisps and drinks 400 gallons of lager beer every evening.

In addition, the survey shows that poor people on the whole are less well off materially than rich people.

Amazing

Another myth exploded by the survey is the so-called North/South divide.

For instance, the figures show that someone earning £70,000 a year in Middlesborough is actually better off than someone earning £500 a year in Wimbledon.

Appalling

However there is a darker side to the new soaraway Britain which cannot be laid at the door of the wonderful Mrs Thatcher, God bless her.

The number of children born in wedlock fell from 856,000 in 1972 to only 3 last year — while more teenagers are engaging in pre-marital smoking than at any time before.

However there is no need to be depressed. Last year Customs men seized a record 50 million tons of heroin, cocaine and foam-filled sofas at Britain's ports, with a street value of £2,897 billion.

There was also a record number of items on the BBC news showing Customs men holding up plastic bags, with the word "Reconstruction" printed at the bottom of the screen.

(That's enough statistics. Ed.)

The Glorious Twelfth

Max Hastings
Editor of The Daily Telegraph

The Glorious Twelfth is here again, a red-letter day in every sportsman's calendar.

Personally, I cannot think of any more exhilirating thought than to be striding through the rain-sodden heather, at 4 o'clock in the morning, straining every nerve to catch sight of one's elusive prey.

For mile after mile, the bleak moorland stretches away to the horizon. There is not another human being in sight, apart from my faithful "ghillie" McWheatcroft and seventy-three Eurobond dealers who have each paid £50,000 for the privilege of a day's shooting alongside such traditional figures as myself and our genial host Lord Hitachi and his lovely wife, the Lady Mitsubisha.

Could there be any finer way than this, I think to myself, to celebrate the anniversary of the bombing of Hiroshima? *(Cont. p.94)*

"This will be your room. They'll ring if they want anything. . .''

Lot three

Sale of very fine
20th Century Pop Memorabilia
— the property of Mr Elton John Esq.
28 February 1988. 10.30 a.m.

THE LOTS

1. First Division football club (Watford), currently bottom of table. Includes various boots, striped shirts and tubes of "Deep Heat" linament cream rub.

2. Gold lame bowler hat with matching glasses and leotard. Designed by Monsieur Julian of Neasden.

3. Pink crocodile-skin platform shoes with powder-blue laces by Maurice and Clive of "The Boot Exchange", Solihull.

4. Diamante baby grand piano with matching stool and piano tuner (Robin). The work of Alessandro Closetti of Amsterdam (1973).

5. Assortment of high-quality hair-pieces in natural colours, by Baldo (Wigs) of Covent Garden.

6. Collection of classic Long-Playing Gramophone Records including works by Miss Shirley Bassey, Miss Barbra Streisand, Miss Elizabeth Minelli, Miss Marilyn Monroe and Miss Judith Garland.

7. Original Sheet Music from various Broadway musicals, namely "Goodnight, Lullaby Baby" *(Yonty Moonstein and Hal Moose, 1935)*, "Turn On The Light, Tootsie" *(Al Yonty and Moose Halstein, 1936)* and "Feets A-Tappin'" *(Moosey Yonstein and Hal Al, 1937)*.
   (That's enough old junk — Ed.)

SOTHEBY'S
FOUNDED 1744

A Doctor writes

As a doctor, I am often asked why some women these days seem to have become obsessively concerned with keeping things tidy.

Well, the simple answer is that these poor women have become victims of the condition known to the medical profession as "obsessional neurosis" (or *Thatcheritis*).

What happens is that the Prime Minister suddenly wakes up in the morning with a vision of the whole country becoming submerged under a tide of rubbish.

She is driven by an insane compulsion to rush around "cleaning everything up" — and in the latter stages of the disease this may even involve her in having to "create" her own "mess" in order to clean it up again.

My picture shows a particularly sad example, of a 62-year-old career woman in St James's Park, "picking up" piles of rubbish which only a few minutes before had been thrown down by herself.

Many such women can be seen in parks all over Britain, although most of them are not the Prime Minister.

If you personally are worried about the problem of "obsessional neurosis", vote Labour.

© A. Doctor.

THIS MAN NEEDS YOUR HELP

An Appeal By the British
"Elephant Man Disease" Foundation
Patron: John Hurt

Elephant Man's Disease (or *Yobbitis Cannabensis*) is a terrible scourge now known to affect one in every 56 million of the population.

Victims of this fearful affliction suffer from continual attacks on other people by themselves. They often find themselves sitting on aeroplanes or quietly walking from John O'Groats to Land's End when they feel the uncontrollable urge to have a few beers and start a fight.

After a while they find it very hard to hold down a steady job, particularly with Queensland, Somerset or England.

In the final stages of the disease they feel driven to surround themselves with circus elephants and walk across the Alps (hence the name of the disease).

There is no known cure for this affliction, which is why we desperately need your money.

Please make cheques payable to John Hurt, Coach and Horses, Greek Street, London (or just give them to the Hon. Treasurer, Jeffrey Bernard).

─────────── Late Score ───────────

FIRST INNINGS
I.T. Botham, not out . . . . 125 miles
Batperson the Elephant, retired hurt . . . . 2 miles
John Hurt, retired drunk . . . . 2 vodkas
Mrs K. Botham, retired to England . . . . 6 miles
Nellie the Elephant, packed trunk, off to join Circus . . . . .
. . . . .10 miles
Eddie the Eagle . . . . 72 yards (British record)
Eddie the Elephant . . . . rest in peace
(*That's enough elephants — Eddie the Editor.*)

MONDAY PAGE

Second time round —it can work

Conventional wisdom would have it that the odds are stacked against a second marriage working. But is this really true? Last week I travelled to Scotland to meet a middle-aged man who despite the failure of a previous marriage has boldly taken the plunge again and is confident that his new relationship will be a success.

> "I thought
> I could never
> go through it all again
> but now I feel
> I can see a real future
> for us."

David is 49, a quietly spoken Scottish Leader of the Liberal Party who until recently was married to the glamorous David Owen.

"It was great at the start and it never occurred to me that one day I would wake up and realize that David and I had nothing in common."

Hearing him talk, there was no sense of the bitterness one normally finds in separated couples. It suggested a man who had learnt a great deal about himself and allowed the hurt to run its course rather than letting it fester.

"Yes it *was* painful," he admitted, "But I was determined not to be dragged down by the whole thing. Life has to go on."

And it certainly has for David who has found a new partner in the softly spoken Scottish Leader of the Social Democratic Party, Robert Maclennan.

Two years older than David, he bears a striking resemblance to David's former companion. Rob explained to me: "The trouble last time was that David desperately wanted a merger and David wouldn't have one and obviously it caused a lot of unhappiness."

Robert, on the other hand, recognizes the need for a couple to have a merger and already they are planning to have one in the spring.

So will they prove the experts wrong? Given their enthusiasm and their obvious affection for one another the chances are that the whole thing will be a complete disaster.

Next week: David and Rosie: Is Love Enough?
© Times Filler Feature Productions 1987.

**The Monday Pages
Edited by
Sally Lymeswold**

Your TV tonight

The new Doctor: "I see him as a bit of a joke."

7.30 Dr Whohe

Yes, the ever-popular Doctor is back, this time in a new incarnation as the former leader of the Social Democratic Party. David Owen is the Doctor. Rosie Barnes is his young pretty assistant. In the coming series he takes on the combined forces of evil Time Lord, Lord Tordoff (Liberal) and the Cyrilsmorg Monster. Does the Doctor have a hope against these enemies? No.

Part 1: The Revenge of the Shirls.
CAST IN FULL
Dr Whohe . . . . DAVID OWEN
Rosie Barnes . . . . . . BONNIE LANGFORD
Lord Tordoff . LORD OLIVIER *(Hologram)*
Shirley Williams . . PRUNELLA SCALES
Smorg . . . . LORD GOODMAN
Man in Telephone Box . . GAVIN STAMP
Man in Tardis . . DAVID FROST
(Dr Whohe theme song by Andrew Lloyd-George and Tommy Steel)

"Take an epistle to the Thessalonians, Miss Jones"

Maggie unveils plan to "save inner cities"

by Our Inner City Staff
D. Kay and Joanna Slumley

Billions of pounds are not to be spent by the Government in a radical 47-point plan to rescue Britain's inner cities from the clutches of the Labour Party, whoops, spiral of urban decay, graffiti, tower blocks, black people, end of civilisation, that sort of thing.

Mrs Thatcher has thrown all the weight of her handbag behind the new 97-point plan which was launched yesterday by a team of 17 Cabinet Ministers at a South London Holiday Inn Conference Centre.

Suit to Kill

As a Royal Marines band played the *Eddie Edwards March* and laser beams created the logo of the Tories' Save Inner Cities from Ken (SICK) campaign, mini-skirted "Thatcherites" handed out glossy brochures and "information kits" to the assembled hacks, toadies and freeloaders (*Shurely, gentlemen of the presh? W.D.*).

Lord Suit of Grantham then burst through a flaming hoop, dressed only in a three-piece suit, to unveil the key features of the Government's 138-point plan.

■ ENTERPRISE Initiative Zones to be set up wherever there is a chance of getting a spot of tax relief for the friends of Lord Suit.

■ VALLEY Initiative Towns to be designated in all areas where unemployment is above the level of 100 per cent or not as the case may be. Precisely what these are has yet to be revealed or, for that matter, worked out.

■ A NATIONWIDE crash programme of Working Ministerial Breakfast Action Teams (WOMBATS) to be sent out to set up Enterprise Cells at the interface of local and national business initiatives in response to a market-oriented revival strategy, etc.

These breakfasts, which will be held in Dragonara hotels, will consist of the following items:

MENU

INNER CITY SIZZLER

Suit de Jour Lord Young
or
Young's Potted Suits

Old Thatcher's Load of Tripe
(this special confection has been cooked up by top chef Tim Bell to give off the rich aroma of rotten eggs)

From The Trolley
Central Office Selection of Humbugs

Lemon Hurd Meringue Pie

School announcements
St Cake's School

Channon Term opened on 11 January. There are 3,819 boys in the school and 5 girls. Hang-Seng Index (Waldegrave's) is Keeper of the Sheaths. N.D.B. Longbond (Mellor's) is Deputy Blazer. P.D.Q. Desktop-Publisher (Rifkind's) is Captain of the Runs. Mr P.I.E Cubmaster has had to retire from the staff for personal reasons, and his place as Moral Tutor will be taken by Prebendary F.B. Grope. Dr L.S.E. Traumer has joined the staff as the school's first full-time Stress Counsellor. Nimby's will be run over Ridley's Meadow on 1 March. There will be a performance of Dennis Plodder's *The Whingeing Playwright* in the Ayckbourn Theatre on 24 March. Examinations for the Semtex Science Scholarship take place in the Saatchi Library on 28 March. Ecstasies will be on 1 April. The O.C. Squash Society will meet for its annual dinner at the Carrington Club, Purley Way, on 7 April. Tickets from the Secretary, Mr R.C. Showergel, 24 Beezer Grove, Peterborough.

GLEN ELTON LIVE

Fleet Street's Alternative Big-Mouth!

SO MRS Thatch is going to see the inner cities! Things are bad enough there without Thatch coming along thank you very much (bit of politics, don't tell Normo Tebbs or he'll be round with a sledgehammer! Right!!).

SCIENTISTS! Doncha just hate 'em!! OK so they came up with the toothbrush but don't forget Hiroshima!! OK!!

People have to stand up for their rights

SO THE Pope says "Buenos Dias" to the wet-backs — Big deal!! Why doesn't the old Papal Nunce cut out the Bull (geddit?!!) and pop on a condom to give us all an example!? OK?!

CAPTAIN BOB!? Isn't he great? I think someone should give him a peerage! Wake up Thatch!?! Know what I mean?!!

Here they are — Glen's non-sexist lovelies!?!!!
Linda Bellos! Crazy name but a totally dedicated Lambeth politician!?!
Diane Abbot?!? Great — saw you on *Question Time*, you really gave Thatch a rough ride!?! I'm Diane to meet yer (geddit?!).
Mary Kenny *(Shurely shome mishtake. Ed.).*
My name's Glen Elton, Goodnight.

Watch out for Benny Green on SATURDAY!?

Wright Case
Maggie appeals to God

by Our Court Staff
Raunchtime O'Bonk

Following her latest series of defeats in the courts of Australia, Britain, Hong Kong and the UN, Mrs Thatcher is planning to appeal to the highest authority of all in her attempt to stop the last three people in the world who haven't yet read *Spycatcher* from seeing it.

The Prime Minister is to send her special envoy, Dr Roald Runcie, to the top of Mount Sinai to plead her case before the Almighty.

"If He won't listen," she screamed, "then I shall have to go to an even higher authority — myself."

PHONE SENSATION

by Our Telecommunications Staff *Bill Toolarge*

IN A shock interview last night the former head of British Telecom, Sir George Jeffbinin, denied that his sudden resignation had anything to do with complaints about the quality of BT service. **Speaking from his home in Oxfordshire he told me:**

"British Telecom is one of the shining examples of privatisation in this country and standards . . . so I'll pick up Aunt Enid from Shipton and we'll drive down on the Tuesday . . . Hello Hello . . . Get off the line will you? As I was saying, the Telecom monopoly has made . . . eight fifty-two precisely — Beep, Beep, Beep . . . Is that Ray? I'm not sure about driving, Enid tends to get car sick in the Allegro . . . This is the Lenny Loony Laugh Line featuring the zany madcap voices of . . . The benefits of high technology and a fair price structure has ensured that the consumer . . .

I'm not wearing any knickers and I'm a traffic warden from Bracknell . . . Roger Sunray Violet Tango — Constable Willis proceeding to Cumberland Avenue for routine . . . so that's two No. 25s with sweet and sour sauce and prawn crackers. About twenty minutes? Thanks . . . All lines from everywhere are engaged. Please try later . . . which is in effect why there is no connection between recent criticism of the company and my own sacking."

Sir George Jeffbinin is 107.

Ten things you didn't know about Bonking

A STAR/SUN/MIRROR EXCLUSIVE

BONKING!!!

1. It sells newspapers
2. It's great.
3. Everyone's talking about it.
4. Everyone's doing it.
5. It's raunchy.
6. It's the greatest new buzz word since raunchy.
7. . . . Er . . .
8. . . . that's it.

ON OTHER PAGES

My Torrid Bonking Nights With Raunchy Blonde Topless Barmaid Lynne by Sir Jock Bruce-Gardyne — p6 *(Shorley shome mishtake? Ed.)*

"Burton's Bonking Boss Did It 50 Times A Night" Claims A Thick Liverpudlian 16-year old Slag Who Has Been Given £500 by Us to Pose Topless on Page 7.

"Smoking Helps You Bonk Longer" — *Dr Madeupname* — *p8*

Unfunny Cartoon by Bonk — p9

Alternative Rocky Horror Service Book

— *No.94* —

Service Of Thanksgiving For The Receipt Of Funds By A Cathedral Church From An Well-Known Personality In The Aftermath Of A Libel Action.

THE PRESIDENT: Brethren, we are gathered here to give thanks for the generous gift of £— *(the sum shall be named, if it is in six figures)*. Who giveth this cheque for our restoration fund?
THE DONOR *(J. Archer, for it is he):* I do.

There may then be an "photo opportunity" on the Chancel steps when the Donor shall pose in the act of handing over the Cheque to the Dean.

THE PRESIDENT: Let us pray.
THE CONGREGATION: Do we have to?
THE PRESIDENT: I'm afraid we do, but I assure you that it won't take long and then we can all go and have coffee in the crypt.

THE PRAYER OF HUMBLE ACCESS CARD

We give thanks for this gift of libel damages which has been so generously bestowed upon us by thy servant J—. We do not wish to go into the rights and wrongs of the painful case all over again, for as Our Lord said: "Never look a gift horse in the mouth." (*Rocky Horror Bible*, Matt 5:3-4). But suffice it to say that as soon as this cheque is cleared, we shall be spending it on turning the Lady Chapel into an disco.

THE PRESIDENT: And now all shall sing the Hymn on the service sheet "All we like sheep have read his books".

Un Taxi-driver écrit

Chaque semaine un fameux taxi-driver ecrit sur un topic d'importance.
Cette semaine:

Jean Marie Le Pen (Numero 6730211)

Les Juifs! Marquez mon mots, monsieur, Ils ont un bloody nerve n'est-ce pas?

J'ai dit seulement que les gas-chambers sont un mere detail dans la guerre et le prochain thing you know, Ils sont calling moi un fasciste!!

Blimey! Si vous demande a moi, Hitler a eu le right idea, guvnor. Stringez-les-up! C'est le seul langue qu'ils comprement ces gens la.

J'ai eu le late Rudolph Hess dans la derriere de mon cab un fois.

© *M.Kington L'independent* *(Le Journal de annee)*

Next Week:
Alfie Sherman
(Cab No. 3724678)
Censorship at the Tory Conference

Jack and Jill–
It must never happen again

By Everyone In Fleet Street and TV and Radio's Brian Bighead.

Jack and Jill —
an artist's impression.

"Yes, they do have a dog next door but I have been assured he doesn't bark"

■ **As the nation reeled yesterday from the shocking news of the tragedy in which two youngsters fell down a hill, one severely breaking his crown and the other, according to an eyewitness, "tumbling after", MPs were demanding "a full inquiry" into how the tragedy had been allowed to occur.**

Mr Anthony Beaumont-Quote, Tory MP for Outrage-on-the-Box, said last night: "All the indications we have suggest that these unfortunate children were totally unsupervised.

"We must consider whether in future, when children take part in these water-fetching leisure activities, they ought not to be supervised by at least five fully-qualified adults for each child."

Child Abuse

Experts had hoped that procedures had been tightened up following the tragic Humpty Dumpty incident some years ago, when an unsupervised egg had fallen from a wall.

Since then, under guidelines issued by local authorities, eggs have only been permitted to sit on walls six inches (or 14 centimetres) high, and it has become a statutory requirement that in all such cases a detachment of trained King's Horses and Men should be standing by in case of emergency.

Beyond the Pail

But, now, only three years later, we have the same sickening lack of proper safeguards, which lead to children being put needlessly at risk.

Among the many demands which were being made yesterday by MPs, social workers, the teaching unions and experts on the *Today* programme were:

● A crash programme to provide proper barriers at danger points on all hills;

● An end to the siting of water-gathering facilities in hilltop situations;

● The provision of new hazard-free pail equipment, as is recommended by the EEC Commission On Safeguards For Juvenile Employees In Water-Fetching Industries (1986);

● Enormous articles in all newspapers asking Why Oh Why Must These Tragedies Go On Happening?

ON OTHER PAGES

Glenda Slag on The Terrible Agony of Jack and Jill's Parents.

Paul Johnson on Why Mrs Thatcher Is Not To Blame.

What Happens When We Cry by **Oliver Gillie**, Medical Correspondent of the Year.

I Blame No One, say parents, and nobody listens   p. 94.

"Mind if we join you?"

<u>WHAT YOU</u> <u>WILL SEE!</u>

IT'S THE HANZZZARD HALF HOUR

—— STARRING ——

THATCH

THE SUPREME RULER OF THE UNIVERSE AS HERSELF

—— AND ——

KINNOCHIO

THE WELSH WINDBAG AS NOT HIMSELF

*PLUS FULL SUPPORTING CAST OF RED-FACED MEN
MAKING SILLY NOISES AND WAVING PIECES OF PAPER*

—— *(MUSIC AND CREDITS)* ——

VOICE OVER: And now we go over live to the House of Commons for today's episode of *Today In Parliament.*

(CAPTION: 2.15. The Televising Of The House Of Commons Enabling Bill [Second Reading])

MR A. GREYMAN *(Publicity-on-the-Brain, Con):* Will the Prime Minister not agree. . .

MRS THATCH *(Compleat, Con):* No, she bloody well won't.

MR SPEAKER: Order, order, we are on television, you know. Hello Mum.

MR GREYMAN: I would move that the time has now come for this House to accept that the introduction of television cameras would be a vital step forward to the widening of democratic accessibility. . .

(Cries of "Get on with it!")

GREYMAN: Hullo, mother, if you're watching.

THATCH: The House will recognise that I have made my position absolutely clear, that this is a totally free vote and that anyone who votes against me will be in deep trouble.

(Labour jeers and cries of "Hullo, darling, I'll be home at seven, put the quiche in the microwave.")

KINNOCK *(Bedwetty, Lab):* Will the Right Honourable Lady not agree that

the real, true, and truly real reason she objects to TV in the House is that she is scared of letting people see the real reality of what goes on in this place day after day, namely the horrible, humiliating and horribly humiliating sight of her shouting me down every

time I try to ask her a perfectly straightforward and straightforwardly perfect question?

(Uproar, cries of "Which camera is on?")

SIR BUFTON TUFTON *(Lymeswold, Con):* Would the Prime Minister not agree that the ancient dignity of this ancient Mother of Parliaments (hic), this sheptic isle, thish jewel in the crown, where wash I?, oh yesh, it would be a shad day (hic) if my constituents, or indeed my ancient and venerable Aunt Gwen (Hullo there, Auntie!), were able to pry into the privacy of Honourable Members after lunch when they might, for no reason of their own, be completely pissed.

(Cries of "Cut", "Half-Cut", "Completely Cut")

MR AUSTIN ROVER *(Grimsbore, Lab):* Surely the point is that those of us who have been on television a great deal want to be on it again even more often, preferably every day, and just because some Honourable Members haven't been professional presenters and know that they will look stupid and amateurish doesn't mean to say that they have the right to stop ordinary working men and women from being able to see the democratic

process actually at work. And may I just conclude by saying "Hullo, mum"?

MR NORMO TEBBS *(Bonkers, Con)*: Mr Speaker, I have never heard so much unadulterated toshwash in my whole life as I have heard from Labour speakers this afternoon. As My Right Honourable Friend the Prime Minister has so wisely said. . .

THATCH: You're still fired, Tebbo.

TEBBS: . . . this is not in any way a party matter. But we all know what will happen once the cameras are in. We'll see nothing but loony left lesbians abseiling in and out of this chamber, making a complete mockery of everything that this government is trying to do to make this country great again.

(Tory cheers. Tory lesbians abseil into chamber demonstrating in favour of Clause 28. Cries of "Hullo, One-Parent Mum")

TEBBS: As I was saying, the real problem will be the blatant bias of the BBC. Can't you just imagine how night after night we shall have the likes of Kate Adie distorting what really goes on in this House and turning it into propaganda for Colonel Gaddafi and her other Marxist friends?

(Tory cheers, Labour boos)

DR DEATH *(Brylcreem, SDP-in-Exile)*: As the Supreme Ruler of the One and Only True Council for Social Democratic Owenism. . .

MR DENNIS BOLSOVER *(Skinner, Lab)*: Siddown, toffee-nose.

DEATH: . . . we have a clear duty to the 27 million people who voted Social Democrat at the last election to ensure that these proceedings are made as public as possible, using all the technology available. The public are not fools, and I submit that when they see on the screens the behaviour of certain loutish elements in this House and when they compare it to the statesman-like demeanour of certain other Members who have held high office as Foreign Secretary, for example, they will at once recognise that I am not totally washed up.

(SDP cheer [Rosie Barnes])

TAM DALYELL *(Binns, Lab)*: Would the Rt Hon Lady not agree that the government's vicious and brutal cover-up of the Stalker enquiry into the sinking of the Belgrano is nothing more than yet another attempt to cover up the fact

that MI5 framed the "Birmingham Six". Hullo, mater!

SPEAKER: And now a look at the Weatherall.

(House empties)

VOICE OVER: And now we go over live to the General Synod for its historic debate on "The Church In Crisis".

(Cut to a lot of vicars asleep)

BISHOP OF CONDOM: I would now like to draw the attention of the Synod to what all Christians must recognise as the gravest threat facing our civilisation today — the Poll Tax.

(Cries of "Yea, yea, verily" and "In a very real sense, you are right")

BISHOP UPTON O'GOOD: I am sure that we all deplore the shocking and immoral introduction of this wicked Bill which has such horrifying implications for our whole community. I would particularly draw the attention of the Synod to Clause 14, Subsection 12, relating to the regional adjustment provisions of the business

rate element of the Community Charge. I am sure that we are all aware that even a two per cent marginal adjustment would produce anomalies here which should not be tolerated by any Christian society.

ALL: Z-z-z-z. . .

ARCHBISHOP OF CANTERBURY: Let us pray.

ALL: No, let us carry on talking about the poll tax. What do you think this is — a vicarage tea party? Are we on television?

REV. TREV OUTREACH: I am really shocked that you're all going on about the boring old poll tax when the real crisis confronting all Christians today is Clause 28.

(Hundreds of straight vicars abseil down into chamber, demanding equal rights. Synod breaks for sherry)

ON OTHER PAGES
Why Oh Why Can't I Be Archbishop of Canterbury? asks John Selwyn Gumboot.

KEVIN WOODCOCK

THE GREATEST MAN WHO EVER LIVED IN THE HISTORY OF THE WORLD

As told to JOE HAINES by Robert Maxwell

SEVERAL books are to be published shortly, purporting to tell the life story of the amazing war hero, businessman and communications genius Robert Maxwell.

They will be filled with half-truths, smears and distortions. Only one will be complete balls from start to finish.

This is it.

Maxwell presents OBEs to the Fabs

Maxwell and Her Majesty the Queen

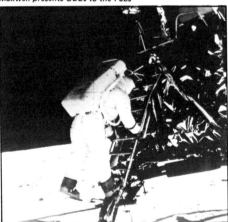

Maxwell lands on the Moon

The incredible boy wonder from Braunnöse

IT IS amazing to think that when he was born in the little Czech village of Perga-monice (today Maxwell-grad) almost no one knew who he was.

Yet today he is the most famous man in the world — and rightly so.

It is said that at the moment of his birth in 1923 local shepherds saw a bright light in the sky above the humble house where his mother and father lived.

When he was five, the village was threatened by a landslide when the whole mountain above it began to slide down onto the hundreds of houses.

The lives of thousands were threatened. It was a tense moment.

But fortunately for them they had in their midst the mild-mannered bespectacled little boy, Clark Hoch, who with one hand held up the whole mountain and saved the village from disaster.

Many were the heroic tales that were told of young Supermax, as his school-friends were quick to dub him, when he told them to.

Once giant wolves invaded the village and would have eaten alive every toddler in the place, if the young Czech superhero had not spoken to the wolves in their own tongue, saying "Be at peace, brothers, and go home."

It was an early example of the astonishing communi-cations skills that were later to make St Maxwell of Assisi a legend in his own lifetime.

ABOUT THE AUTHOR

JOE HAINES is one of the most distinguished syco-phants in Britain today. For many years he worked as chief toady to Lord Wislon of Revolting. Now he has been paid a lot of money to write this drivel about another fat old fraud.

Now read on.

The Pope pays homage to Maxwell

How he won the war single handed

In 1939 the war clouds loomed over Europe. Soon only one thing stood between Hitler and total world domination. His name was Robert Maxwell.

When the Nazis entered Czechoslovakia in the spring of 1935, the 12-year-old Maxwell quickly formed a one-man partisan resistance movement that was described by German General Ludicrous von Kennedy as "the most efficient fighting machine ever known to mankind — and that includes the Wehrmacht".

Luckily for Britain, in 1941 Maxwell was able to swim across the North Sea and offer his services to Winston Churchill.

Britain's wartime premier had no doubt about the quality of the young man who stood before him.

"My boy," he said in his familiar bulldog tones, "you are the only man who can lead the free world to victory."

Soon, with his trademark beret with its two badges, Field-Marshal Maxwell of Alamein became the best-loved war leader in the allied armies, and single-handedly turned the tide of the war.

In 1943 it was Italy. In 1944 it was Normandy. By 1945 Maxwell had invented the atom bomb and dropped it on the Japanese.

HOW MAXWELL WON THE V.C.

IN July 1944, as allied troops became bogged down in Normandy, it seemed that defeat was staring them in the face.

And then, near the tiny village of Molloy St Michel, Maxwell crawled under heavy fire to a nearby Panzer tank, killed the five members of the crew with his bare hands, drove the tank to Berlin, and set fire to Hitler's bunker, thus ending the war.

Not surprisingly, for this feat of astonishing bravery Maxwell was awarded the VC and bar — the only man in history ever to have received this honour.

This story has never been told until now, due to the modesty of the quiet hero, who disarmingly said to me: "It was nothing. Put it in your book or you'll be fired."

How Maxwell became the richest man in the world

Back in civilian life, Maxwell turned his dazzling array of talents to a wide variety of careers, in each one of which he shone.

In 1949 he became a brain surgeon, inventing the famous "Bobotomy" — an operation which can overnight transform a brilliantly clever man into a time-serving cabbage. Among the beneficiaries of this breakthrough is former ambassador Sir Peter Jaybotham.

In 1953 Maxwell led his own non-league football club, Maxchester Rovers, to an astonishing FA Cup Final victory.

Maxchester were 10 goals down with only three minutes to go.

Although Bob was the only man left on the field, he was undaunted.

His lightning series of quadruple hat-tricks in the last second not only secured the Cup for the Rovers but earned him the nickname "The Wizard of Drivel".

In the same year he rode the winner of the Derby, became the first man to climb Everest, and also officiated at the Coronation of Her Majesty the Queen.

It is a little known fact that he gave the Queen all her money.

THE WOMEN WHO LOVED HIM

MANY beautiful women have loved Robert Maxwell to distraction.

Among those who have thrown themselves at his feet and begged him to marry them are:

- Marilyn Monroe
- Greta Garbo
- Rita Hayworth
- Marlene Dietrich
- Margaret Drabble

But Maxwell has remained true to his childhood sweetheart, Peta Jay.

Today a whole team of secretaries works round the clock, just answering the millions of letters sent to Maxwell by lovesick, beautiful women from all over the world.

Maxwell wins the Cup

In tomorrow's Mirror:
HOW Maxwell saved millions from famine in Ethiopia and won the Nobel Peace Prize.

In the day after's Mirror:
MAXWELL finds a cure for AIDS and ends the Cold War with a phone call to his old friend Gorbachov.

In the day after that's Mirror:
HOW Maxwell brought lasting peace and harmony to mankind.

The day after that:
HOW the Daily Mirror went bankrupt.

WINTER SPORTS

Eddie goes for gold!

by Our Man in Calgary
Lunchtime O'Lympics

He may be a flop, a non-starter, a Loser with a capital L, but, say what you like, Britain's Eddie "The Shah" has got a heart as big as the Rocky Mountains.

Who else would launch a national newspaper with no experience apart from a couple of trial runs with a free sheet in Warrington? But that's exactly what this shy 20-stone British competitor did — and the crowd loved it! Or rather they didn't.

YES, TODAY'S MAN

As he launched himself down the steep circulation slope, the world held its breath. For a second it looked as though the man they were already calling Eddie "The Shah", the man on whom all Britain had pinned their hopes, was going to take off. But then tragedy struck and Eddie fell off the end and plummeted to the bottom.

Amazingly, this plucky plasterer from Plumstead *(Shurely shome mishtake? Ed)* fell on his feet. Advertising agencies loved him. Overnight his name became synonymous with failure, as one man from top agency Bogleby Hagell & Pratt explained:

"There's nothing the Brits love more than a man who makes a complete balls-up of everything. We're thinking seriously about using him to advertise his next newspaper."

LAST POST

Undeterred by his previous performance, Eddie is talking about having another attempt to prove that he is not just the gormless idiot that the newspapers have made him out to be. To his critics he has only this to say: "Don't write me off. I'll do that myself."

Brian MacArthur is 79.

"Good news - first indications from the results of your tests suggest that you haven't gone permanently blind"

*"I'm the only prick **outside** the Groucho"*

From *Naked London*, published by Quartet (prop. Naim Attallah-Disgusting)

A Sunday WasteofTimes Special Offer

Now you too can own an original David Cockney

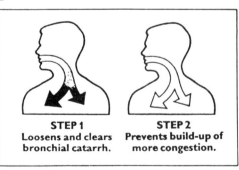

STEP 1
Loosens and clears bronchial catarrh.

STEP 2
Prevents build-up of more congestion.

Hackney's work usually costs a fortune. Last week, for instance, a Japanese businessman bought his *Boy With No Clothes On* for 90 million yen. Now all that has changed.

The picture above is a genuine Cockeye print. It isn't any good, but it *is* genuine.

Just tear it out, get one of your kids to colour it in with a felt-tip pen, and stick it in a frame labelled *Boy With Catarrh*.

Hey Presto! You're a millionaire!

THE BOOK OF SHAMIR

Chapter 95.

1. And, in his wisdom, Shamir said unto the children of Israel: "Hearken unto me, for, behold, I have taken counsel of myself and it has been revealed unto me by the Lord how we shall bring peace to all the land of Israel, even unto the Strip of Gaza and the land of the West Bank that is called 'Occupied Territories'.
2. "Go forth, even unto the forests of Lebanon, and find there the great cedars, yea even the cedars of Lebanon.
3. "And ye are to hew down the cedars and make unto yourself an multitude of mighty clubs, so many that no man may count them, more than are the sands of the beaches of Eilat, which is called Israel's premier tourist resort, like unto the land of Ben-i-dorm and Torre-mol-in-os, wherein may be beheld gorgeous, pouting daughters of Israel clad only in *(Get on with it – God)*"
4. And when the clubs had been fashioned, each one even an cubit in length, the children of Israel went forth into the dwellings of the Arab-ites in the land of Gaza and there they did set about the smiting of the Arab-ites, showing unto them no mercy.
5. And it was about the first hour of the day that the smiting began. And Shamir looked upon the smiting and saw that it was good.
6. And the smiting continued even unto the going down of the sun.
7. And the evening and the morning was the first day.
8. And so it continued, even as Shamir had commanded. For he said "Blessed are those that smite in my name, for they shall truly be called the peacemakers."
9. And Shamir decreed that the smiting should continue until the Arab-ites and the Araf-ites should strike their tents and steal away from the borders of Israel, even unto the far-off lands of the other Arab-ites who do not want them either.
10. And far off, in the land of Man-hat-tan, there dwelt a certain Israelite whose name was Woo-dy Al-len.
11. And he cried aloud in a small nervous voice: "Excuse me, guys, I cannot believe what I am seeing on NBC. Like war is wrong, isn't it, guys? I mean, jeez."
12. But Shamir hearkened not unto the plea of Woo-dy, which was unto him like the song of the locust in the noonday sun, as it singeth afar off in the valley of Herman.
13. For he heareth it not.
14. And lo, all the peoples of the world spake out with one voice and cried unto Shamir: "The smiting must stop. It hath gone far enough."
15. And Shamir heard them not, for, lo, his heart was hardened like unto the unripe avocado that lieth upon the shelf of Marks and Spencer.
16. And, lo, the smiting continued, even unto page 94.

EYE STYLE

Introducing
▪THE▪YEPPIES▪

BRITAIN'S newest socio-economic group. Here for the first time you can get the low-down on tomorrow's biggest trend.

WHO are they?

► Yeppies are features editors and writers who work for national newspapers.

WHERE do you find them?

► You find them on papers like *The Times*, the *Mail*, the *Standard* and practically everywhere else.

HOW do they get their name?

► Simple. Yeppies are the spineless hacks who, when they are told to go and write a load of drivel about people who live in Battersea and own Filofaxes, say "Yep!"

WHAT do they do?

► Yeppies come up with very weak ideas about decorating houses and driving Porsches and then get fired.

WHERE do they go?

► Yeppies immediately go onto another flagging newspaper to take the job of someone else who has just been fired for writing a lame series of pieces about Compact Discs. They then compile an extremely feeble list of restaurants in Covent Garden and get fired.

WHAT do they do in the evening?

► Having been fired twice, Yeppies go to El Vinos and get completely pissed. While they are there they bump into an Editor of a national newspaper who says, "Do you want a job on our new *Lifestyle* page?" They say "Yep!"

Yeppies are 39.

TRIVIAL PURSUIT

by Simon Greyman

A moving play about a man who goes to Cambridge and spends the next 30 years writing plays about people who go to Cambridge and spend the next 30 years writing plays about people who *(That's enough of people going to Cambridge and writing plays, Ed)*.

Now, for the very second time in the West End, the play nobody wanted to see the first time.

Starring the tall one in the cigar ads who does the building society one as well.

PLUS
the one who was in all those Scottish films.

PLUS
the one who says "bastard" and "willy" on the telly, you know the one.

PLUS
lots of other ones, including the one who does all those impressions of other ones.

"Hurry, Hurry Enfield is much funnier."

The Independent

GNOMIX THEATRE

Pavements to be privatised

by Our Lunatic New Government Measures Staff
Peter J. Walker and Major Roads Boyson

The Government is to sell off Britain's pavements in a £7,000 billion scheme to raise money to give away in the next Budget.

Transport supremo Mr Paul Chinless yesterday detailed the plan to introduce the "Pay-As-You-Walk" pavement to Britain's cities.

Shares will be sold to the public (Kuwait Petroleum Inc) in a newly formed company to be called BP (or British Pavements).

The ownership of all "pedestrian thoroughfares" will be transferred by law to the new company, which will be completely responsible for their future maintenance and upkeep.

"This will save Britain's local authorities an estimated £700 billion a day," Mr Chinstrap lied, "which will be a major contribution to keeping down our disastrous new community charge."

1. SPECIAL new yellow and blue BP "tollbooths" with automatic barriers will be installed on every street corner in Britain.

2. IN order to gain access to the pavements, members of the public will simply have to pay a "reasonable toll fee" (initially estimated at £1.50 per metre, or part of a metre).

3. THE Government is keen to emphasise that there will be no limit to the number of metres that pedestrians can subscribe for at any one time, and members of the walking public will theoretically be able to walk from Land's End to John O'Groats, if they can afford it.

4. TO ensure no "fare dodging" by the lower-waged, special teams of security officials (known as "Walkmen") will be employed by BP to throw non-paying pedestrians into the path of oncoming traffic using the new Executive Gold Card Enterprise Lanes of the new "pay-as-you-drive" roads that the Government is hoping to introduce first.

Mr Paul Chinwag is 23.

The Book of Shamir

Chapter 98:
"The Parable of the One Lost Israeli"

1. And, lo, the children of Israel went forth into the places where there dwelt the Arab-ites and the Araf-ites and all the children of the ungodly.
2. And the children of Israel cried out with a loud voice and said: "Woe unto ye, ye Arab-ites. For ye have lifted up stones and cast them amongst us.
3. "Therefore are we wroth, and ye shall be smitten even as the chaff of the field is beaten out upon the winnowing floor."
4. And the children of Israel rose up and slew the Arab-ites.
5. And they were slain by day and by night: men, women and children, slewn were they all.
6. And the numbers of the slain were first a score, then two score, then three score, then four score, then five score.
7. Until the numbers of the slain reached even unto an hundredfold.
8. And there was among the Arab-ites much wailing and gnashing of teeth.
9. But the children of Israel heard them not, nor did they weary of the smiting.
10. And, lo, it came to pass that on a certain day the Arab-ites slew one of the children of Israel.
11. And it was a very different story.
12. And when these things were told unto Shamir, he rent his garments and cried out with a mighty voice "Ichabod", which is to say: "You bastards, you are really for it this time."
13. And there was great wailing and gnashing of teeth through all the land of Israel.
14. And they said, one unto another: "Who will come to the beaches of Eil-at when they see on *News At Ten* that the sons of Israel are dying, even in their ones?"
15. And Shamir said to the people: "The Lord God hath spoken to me personally, with regard to this one, like unto his servant An-der-ton.
16. "And he hath said: 'Truly is it written that there shall be more wailing and gnashing of teeth over one Israeli soldier who is lost than over ninety-and-nine of the Arab-ites that have been slain."
17. And Shamir went away and ordered that the smiting should be multiplied.
18. For he saith, as the prophet hath written, it is the only language these people understandeth.

To be continued

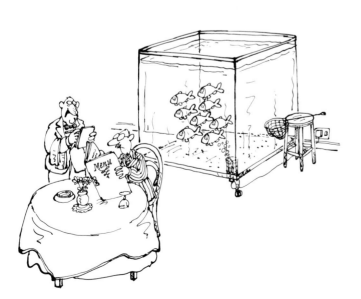

"I'll have the steak"

In an astonishingly frank interview with the Editor of the Daily Mail, Sir David Fester, the Prime Minister speaks as she has never spoken before about her hopes, her fears and her steamy love life (Shome mishtake — shurely you mean "comprehensive schools"?).

MY VISION OF MY BRITAIN

by Margaret Thatcher

TO THE casual observer, Mrs Thatcher might easily have been mistaken for a goddess, with her radiant smile, soothing presence and the unearthly halo of celestial light which shone around her auburn hair.

It would be easy to confuse Mrs Thatcher with Mother Theresa or even Esther Rantzen.

Her incomparable beauty speaks for itself. But this was a woman with her feet firmly planted on my neck.

As she motioned me to a chintz-covered sofa (Andrew Neill), she told me that her mission to transform Britain had only just begun.

When Margaret Roberts Hidla Thatcher first entered the House of Commons in 1959, England was a very different place — a happy, peaceful, friendly land of thatched cottages, Ealing films and smiling, dimple-cheeked milkmaids wandering o'er the lea with their freshly garnered baskets of Ovaltine.

There was not a condom in sight.

Garbage

But then, into this earthly paradise, came the ravening monster of the 'sixties.

Suddenly Harold Wilson was Prime Minister. Gigantic tower blocks suddenly sprouted on every village green.

Crazed gangs of teenagers made shameless love in the streets, while the jungle rhythms of pop music bellowed from a thousand discos.

Crime soared, old ladies were mugged on every street corner, the River Tiber foamed with blood, and witchcraft reigned supreme in every public library.

"That is what the 'sixties were all about, Mr Fester," beamed the saintly Madonna of the Falklands. "Our beautiful, wholesome country was taken over by an alien culture — it was simply horrible.

"But then, in the 'seventies, things got even worse. All our lovely old grammar schools were destroyed by some mad woman who had become Secretary of State for Education."

"You mean Shirley Williams?" I put it to the Prime Minister.

"No, you fool — it was me," she spat, with a touching snarl.

Litter

"And worst of all," the Prime Minister continued, "was the way women forsook their traditional role as homemakers and were turned overnight into wild-eyed, ranting viragos, bent on becoming Prime Minister.

"But all this is going to change, Lord Fester — as you will be when you've printed this article in the *Daily Mail*. My aim is to wipe away every last trace of those horrible 'sixties from the Britain we love."

Her voice rising to a crescendo, she told me in a vibrant contralto: "Nor shall my sword sleep in my hand, Sir David, until I have built Jerusalem in England's green and pleasant belt."

As she ushered me to the door and admitted Brian Walden for the next interview, I felt that I had been privileged to have been given a glimpse of silken thighs encased in satin black silk (*Shurely you mean "a glorious vision of the Britain of tomorrow"? — Sub-Ed*).

© *Lord English-and-proud-of-it, Mailtrash Publications 1988.*

The Book of Shamir

Chapter 105.

1. And, lo, it came to pass that a decree went out from Shamir that all those who dwelt in the land of Israel should go forth to cast their votes, except of course for Arab-ites.
2. And so it was that Shamir and Peres came before the people to see which one they should choose to lead them.
3. For they said: "Shamir is an ex-tre-mist who wishes only to smite the Arab-ites.
4. "Whereas Peres is an mod-er-ate, that is to say one who wishes only to smite the Arab-ites."
5. And they did not know what it was that they should do.
6. Then there arose privily certain Arab-ites and they went up into the land of Jericho and slew a woman, a daughter of Israel, and her children.
7. And there went up from all the children of Israel a great wailing and gnashing of teeth.
8. And Shamir rent his garments and cried: "Woe is me, for now I am bound to win."
9. And the children of Israel cried with one voice: "Woe unto the Arab-ites and the Araf-ites and they that live in the tents of the uncircumcised.
10. "For the wrath of the Lord shall descend upon them like the lightning bolt that striketh the grasshopper of Baby-lon in the heat of the noonday sun."
11. Then went they forth into the land of Jericho and laid waste the orchards and the villages of the Arab-ites, even with bull-dozers.
12. And they took all the men of Jericho into a certain place and did a bit of smiting.
13. And from morning until night the smiting continued.
14. And when they looked upon the lands of the Arab-ites, lo, there was not one banana grove left standing, nor any man of the Arab-ites who remained unsmitten.
15. And the children of Israel looked upon the work they had done and saw that it was good, and that the Arab-ites had been paid out an hundred-fold.
16. For the orange trees of the land of Jericho were laid as flat as the beaches of Ei-lat, where the Sons of Thom were having a little difficulty in selling their winter sun-shine breaks this year for some reason which they could not comprehend.
17. And the boards of Wind-surf lay idle on the sands, and the bowls of salted peanuts at the Sol-o-mon Ho-tel were heaped high, for no one was there to ask for an Mas-ada Daiquiri from Reu-ben, the man who tendeth the bar.
18. And, lo, it came to pass that on the day appointed the children of Israel went up to cast their votes.
19. And when the casting was done, and all the votes had been counted, lo, it appeared that very little had come to pass at all, and they were back where they had begun.
20. For the followers of Shamir and the followers of Peres were equal in number.
21. And the children of Israel beat their breasts and rent their garments, for they knew that the power in the land of Is-rael had passed into the hands of the men with beards and hats who are called many things, but shall be known in this family Bible only as Hatt-ites.
22. And the Hatt-ites rubbed their hands together that such a thing should have befallen them. For now they could issue decrees that no man might drink an milk-shake nor eat a bacon-flavoured crisp on an El-Al flight to New York on a Sat-ur-day, under pain of death.
23. And the people of Israel groaned within themselves.
24. But then the Hatt-ites promised also that there should be more smiting of the Arab-ites than ever before, even an hundredfold when it comes to the smiting.
25. And, when they heard this, the children of Israel cheered up an lot.

Part 48 of Channel 4's 78-part series "That Was The Year That Was".
Red Ludwig — 20 Years On

(Shot of agreeable detached house in respectable suburb of Frankfurt. Mercedes draws up and middle-aged prosperous-looking man holding briefcase gets out)

VOICE OVER: When Red Ludwig led the 72-hour sit-in at the Goethe Polytechnischeschule in Bad Hofmeister in May 1968, it seemed that the world would never be the same again.

For several weeks the whole of Europe held its breath, waiting for Red Ludwig's latest pronouncements.

It was he who gave the worldwide student revolution some of its most powerful slogans — "Make trousers, not love." "Ich bin eine potsmoker." "Shoot the bourgeoisie — it's the only language the pigs understand."

Today, 20 years on, Red Ludwig is a lecturer at the Goethe Polytechnichschule at Bad Hofmeister. He heads the Faculty of 1968 Studies,

1968 RETROSPECTIVE

lecturing on "The Events of 1968" and his own part in them to a new generation of admiring students who were scarcely born when their ageing professor was making history.

(Cut to large, prosperous-looking room where Red Ludwig is being brought enormous plate of wurst by Frau Ludwig)

RED LUDWIG *(speaking between mouthfuls):* Ja, I vould still describe meinself as ein revolutionary socialist und I am still a passionate believer in all the ideals of Marxism/Leninism — nevertheless, von has to say that zis Monsieur Le Pen has many gut ideas.

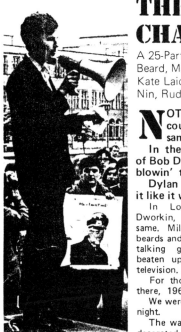

THE YEAR THAT CHANGED THE WORLD

A 25-Part Retrospective on 1968 compiled by Ron Beard, Martin Dope, Kevin Demo, Sid Dreary and Kate Laid with contributions from Jean-Marie Le Nin, Rudy Hitler and Mohammed Ali.

NOTHING after 1968 could ever be the same again.

In the immortal words of Bob Dylan, "the wind is blowin' thru the streets". Dylan was only "telling it like it was".

In London, Paris, New Dworkin, the story was the same. Millions of men with beards and jeans sitting around talking garbage and being beaten up by the police on television.

For those of us who were there, 1968 was really great.

We were on television every night.

The walls of our flats were decorated with the symbols of revolution.

Che Guevara, Ho Chi Minh, Tariq Ali — they were our prophets, leading mankind into a new age on a wave of cheap pot and a chance not to shave for months on end.

And as for the birds, they were fantastic.

It was free love around the clock.

As Dylan said: "The streets are full of people makin' love."

And in Paris, the students joined hands with the workers to bring down the government. Well, nearly.

They were heady days. When anything seemed possible. We were making the future with every stone we tore up from the streets.

As Dylan said: "The streets are full of stones."

And talking of the Stones, they were absolutely great as well.

I went to Hyde Park when they let off all those butterflies.

It was free music, free love and free nights in the nick if you were lucky.

You know, I miss it really. It's hard to imagine that it was only 20 years ago that we were all part of the revolution that changed the world.

Without 1968 the world would be a totally different place.

It would be full of hate, violence and tyranny.

Mind you, I don't rate the Stones like I used to.

As Dylan said: "The streets are full of Mick Jagger and his Rolls-Royce."

That somehow sort of sums up the whole era.

In ten years' time we will look back on 1968 and realise that it was 30 years ago and that it's time for me to write this piece all over again.

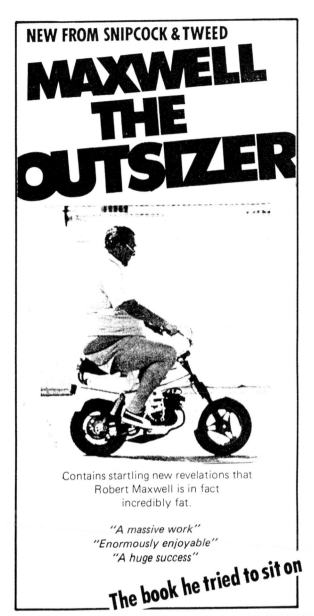

"I wouldn't mind but these are only the popadums"

The Eye says

GOOD ON YER MAGGIE !

IT MAY be a bit overdue, but thank Gawd Mrs Thatcher has got the sense to pay up when it really matters.

We salute the Prime Minister for showing that this country really does care about the hardest-working, most dedicated public servants of all.

They call them "Angels" and they deserve every penny of their rise. For too long they have been overworked and underpaid whilst the whole nation has been crying out for justice for them.

Their professionalism, their devotion and their refusal to take industrial action just proves how lucky we are to have them working for us.

A rise, taking into account the effects of the Budget, of £10,000 a year after tax for the average High Court Judge is no less than his due and is at last a recognition that this Government has got its priorities right.

Hats off to the Judges and God Bless You Ma'am for giving them the whacking increase that they so richly deserve!

"Writ from Maxwell"

RECORDING ANGEL

AIRMAIL

TIM MADDEN

TODAY

. . . and the American long-bond has eased on the Far Eastern markets in late trading. . .

HOBDAY: Thank you, Patrick. And now we return to Moscow where Brian is ready to believe anything he is told. Are you there, Brian?

BIGHEAD: Yes, Peter.

HOBNOB: The news here in London is that the Summit seems to be going pretty well. Is that the way it looks to you in Moscow?

REDBEARD: Well, Peter, the news here in Moscow confirms very much what you're hearing over there in London. The Summit is going very well indeed, so we hear.

HOBJOY: So what you're saying, Brian, if I'm hearing you right, is that the reports we are getting that the Summit is going very well are pretty consistent with what you've been picking up on the ground over there in Moscow? Would that be fair?

BIGWIG: Well, Peter, the feeling here is very much that it is time for *Thought For The Day.*

HOBNAIL: Thank you, Brian. And now it's the Bishop of Flannel, who is here with his friend to make a statement.

BISHOP FLANNEL: Hullo Peter, hullo Brian. You know, some of us are getting pretty fed-up with Mrs Thatcher quoting the Bible all over the place. I mean, anyone can do that — just picking quotes at random to prove a point. It makes you sick. How dare Mrs Thatcher lecture us on how to do our job. Honestly, it's not as though we go round telling her how to run the country, even though she's making such a mess of it. I mean, honestly, that poll tax is a complete disaster. And as for the social security benefit changes, they're plain wicked. I'm all for this individual responsibility she's on about, but the point is that she is individually responsible for everything that's wrong with this country. Isn't that right?

HOBJOB: Thank you, Bishop, and thank you, friend. And now back to Moscow where Brian has been having dinner with a typical Russian family.

REDUNDERTHEBED: The one thing I wanted to do here in Moscow was to meet a completely ordinary Russian couple in the privacy of their own home to ask them to tell me frankly what the ordinary Russian in the street thinks of glasnost and perestroika. Then suddenly, quite out of the blue, I had this telephone call inviting me to drop in at a typical Russian house near the Kremlin.

(Sound of clinking cutlery as servants clear away remains of five-course meal)

FATHEAD: So what we hear in the West about terrible food shortages is all untrue?

RUSSIAN FEMALE VOICE SPEAKING VERY PRECISELY: Under perestroika food production has risen significantly. Last year supplies of food in the Moscow region outstripped demand by 107 per cent.

REDHERRING: That's amazing. Tell me, as an ordinary Russian, do you support what the Party leadership is trying to do, with its policies of glasnost and perestroika?

RUSSIAN MALE VOICE: Yes, we approve totally of the policies of the Party, particularly those of perestroika and glasnost. Another bottle of vodka, Mr Rednose?

BEDSTEAD: Tell me, are you members of the Party yourselves?

RUSSIAN VOICE: Yes, my wife and I have both been life-members of the Communist Party since we were at school.

BEDPAN: That's amazing. And do you hold any rank in the Party?

RUSSIAN VOICE: Da, I am the General Secretary of the Central Praesidium of the Supreme Soviet, and my wife is famous for hating Nancy Reagan.

REDFACE: Thank you, Mr and Mrs Gorbachev.

(Contd. 94kHz)

"It doesn't flower very often but when it does it's quite spectacular"

Glenda Slagg talks to John Mortimer

"Would you like some more champagne?" beamed the brilliant barrister turned bestselling author and playwright. We were sitting in his delightful 17th century Oxfordshire oasthouse on the river near Henley, discussing the new series of *Rumpole* due out later this year. "He's quite a dear, isn't he, old Rumpole, don't you think?" he asked. "Really rather a sweetie." We were looking out over the magnificent garden with its splendid hydrangeas. . . beautiful wife. . . agreeable wines. . . "My father was blind, you know. . ." . . . visits to Tuscany. . . *Brideshead Revisited*. . . Lord Olivier. . . what a sweetie. . . *Paradise Postponed*. . . Michael Hordern. . . what a sweetie. . . Mrs Thatcher. . . what a sweetie. . . whoops. . . terrible old bat. . . I've given up the law, you know. . . novel just out. . . all about Tuscany. . . agreeable wines. . . new series of *Rumpole*. . . partly based on my father. . . a barrister, you know. . . what a sweetie. . . All too soon it was time to leave.

© G. Slagg, Naughtitrash Plc.

Exclusive Serialisation of the Play that no-one's Talking About

Beyond reasonable doubt it's a flop

by Jeffrey Archer

Act II

Scene III

The curtain rises on on the drawing room at the old Vicarage in London. The French windows open onto the garden from where comes the sound of birdsong. It is a lovely spring morning in Autmn.

MRS WOODEN *is sitting at her writing desk. Enter* **MR WOODEN.**

MRS WOODEN: Hello darling.

MR WOODEN: Hello darling.

MRS WOODEN: How was Norfolk?

MR WOODEN: Very flat.(*Audience laughter*)My mother has died.

MRS WOODEN: To loose one parent may be accounted as misfortune. To lose two begins to look like carelessness. (*Audience hysteria*)

MR WOODEN: How did you enjoy the musical last night?

MRS WOODEN: I came out humming the scenery.
(Audience rises in standing ovation lasting 5 minutes)

MR WOODEN: And what did you think of Frank Finlay?

MRS WOODEN: My dear, he ran through the entire gamut of human emotions from A-B.

(That's enough old jokes from other people's plays. Ed.)

TO TRAINS

NORTHERN LINE

FOR YOUR DIS-COMFORT AND INCONVENIENCE WE HAVE SWITCHED OFF ALL THE ESCALATORS

TO ALL READERS

From this week *The New Dullsman* and *Really Boring Weekly* are to merge to form a brand new magazine henceforth to be known as *The New Dullsman and Really Boring Weekly*.

This dramatic change of title reflects a dramatic change of emphasis which will incorporate the best of both periodicals but which will create a radically new and exciting journalistic force.

THIS WEEK

Are Britain's Polytechnics underfunded?

Whither Mitterrand? A nation decides.

No future for the Anglo-Irish Accord?

Crisis in the Town Halls.

Health Auxiliaries — Are they getting a fair deal?

Kinnock under attack — Review or Revision?

PLUS

Hundreds of other quite mindblowingly tedious pieces.

NEW DULLSMAN & REALLY BORING

ON SALE NOW

Civilisation in peril as our culture crumbles

by Sir William Really-Smugg

As I sit down at my agreeable desk to write my regular Tuesday column for the *Indescribablytedious* (a paper I do not have time to read myself, due to my ever-increasing burden of public responsibilities, which now I believe include being Chairman of the Press Council, or is it the Royal Opera House — it makes no difference), I am wondering what on earth I can write about.

It strikes me that my very lack of ideas is a reflection of the vacuity of modern civilisation. Where are Goethe, Shakespeare and Mozart today? Gone forever, and we cannot hope to see their like again. *Ou sont les neiges d'antan?* Never glad confident morning again. Bliss was it in that dawn to be alive. *(Please get on with it, if you would be so kind. A.W-S.)*

Only yesterday I was sitting in my garden in Somerset thinking how very fortunate I am to be a man of Wessex.

The sun may shine on other parts of the world as well, but surely it never shines more brightly than it does on the sleeping fields and agreeable cathedrals of this venerable fiefdom of the free where once King Woosnam was converted to Christianity in the late 6th century by St Hilda of Grantham.

Wessex! The very name is like a great bell tolling down the centuries, calling the men of England back to themselves. The smack of leather on willow, the moan of doves in immemorial elms, the drone of columnists faxing their copy from agreeable Somerset rectories back to the hurly-burly of Londinium. Can we not hear the tramp of Roman legions as their sandals beat a path up the Fosse Way, from ancient Cadbury Camp to the home of Rowntree in Eboracum? When I was in Japan the Rowntree affair was little mentioned *(come on Sir William, it's time for your nap).*

Reprinted from
The Indescribablyinept, 1988

Sooty: "Yes, I took drugs with vice girls"

by Our Filth Staff
Peter Coke and Koo Starkers

A shamefaced Sooty yesterday broke down and confessed that he had "resorted to cocaine and call-girls" in order to alleviate the pressures of his working schedule.

Known to millions as TV's Mr Clean, the fluffy glove puppet with the black ears and the wand looked pale and drawn as he answered questions at his £700,000 hideaway cardboard box in Harry H. Corbett's Wanstead home.

Glove Nest

"You've no idea what it's like at the top. I felt I was being manipulated. I was out of control and it was only a desperate cry for help that led me down the path of drug abuse and fabulous birds in suspender belts."

But not everyone was quick to condemn the much-loved TV idol known to insiders as "Snowy". Sooty's long-term companion, Sweep, has promised to stick by him.

"I know what he's been through, love," he explained to reporters, "and there's no way I'm going to walk out on him now. He's a wonderful, warm and understanding creature who is like so many celebrities these days who get caught with their trousers down and their wand in some very strange places."

Bough Trade

The BBC was quick to deny that Sooty would be dropped from its schedules.

Said a BBC spokesman, Mr A.S. Bestos: "As far as we are concerned what Mr Sooty does in his own time is entirely a matter for him. He has always been a total professional and has never let his drug-taking or whoring affect his performance as a family entertainer. And let me say that he is by no means the only one. After all, they don't call it White City for nothing."

Sooty is 93.

THE Times

Friday, May 13, 1988

THE TRUTH ABOUT "SENORITA FILTH"

Carmen Miranda

by Our Man In Gibraltar
Lunchtime O'Smear

Last night millions of British TV viewers were stunned when Gibraltar housewife Mrs Carmen Proetta claimed to have seen SAS men shooting IRA terrorists.

Mrs Proetta was presented as an ordinary Gibraltar housewife who had actually witnessed the events she described.

In fact, we can reveal, after investigations into Mrs Prostituta's background lasting more than seven seconds, that the so-called "key witness" on Thames TV's disgraceful *Up The IRA* documentary is nothing less than the leading "Satanist" of the Western world.

Myra Hindley

Not only did this self-confessed heroin addict and mass murderer once slaughter babies live on a Spanish TV chat show, she is believed to have single-handedly smuggled the AIDS virus into Britain disguised as "Carlos the Jackal", the notorious international vampire bat.

Known in Gibraltar as "La Dracula", Gibraltarians claim that no one is safe at night as she swoops down from her love nest with the apes on unsuspecting toddlers.

Gibraltarian police sources confirm that Thames TV "must have paid" the Rock's most hated woman "billions of pounds" to peddle her complete farrago of lies to the British media, when we are perfectly capable of making up our own.

"It's desperate, sir - we're down to our last poet!"

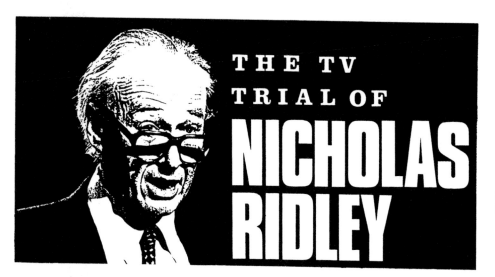

THE TV TRIAL OF NICHOLAS RIDLEY

(Blurred shot of elderly white-haired Nazi walking dog through agreeable Cotswold village)

VOICE OVER: Did this man — or did he not — personally order the shooting down of plans to build four highly desirable "executive-style" Georgian bungalows in his back garden?

(Cut to elderly man wearing Old Etonian tie)

RIDLHEIM: It vos all a long time ago. Surely you cannot expect me to remember the details of what happened in 1985?

(Cut to film of screaming, cheering supporters at Mrs Margaret Hilda Thatcher's triumphant rally at Blackpool in 1985. A uniformed Ridlheim, wearing the distinctive insignia of a top party functionary — blue suit and glasses — is haranguing an ecstatic audience of party faithful)

ADOLF RIDLER: And zat is vy ve are sending ze houses into ze greenbelt. Nuzzink vill stop ze advance of our glorious detached homes into ze green und leafy countryside of Britain. I hereby declare total war on ze craven und despicable armies of so-called conservationism, who are only showing their total selfishness in trying to stop ze onward march of our heroic developers, with their pathetic slogan "Not in Mein Own Backyard" — or Nimby-Pambyism as I like to call it!

(Shot of Mrs Thatcher gazing adoringly up at her favourite son as he receives standing ovation from the audience, who sing "Development Land of Hope and Glory")

GRITTY INVESTIGATIVE STYLE VOICE OVER: Yet our researches show that, at the very moment when Ridlheim was receiving this hysterical adulation, he was sending this letter to the Planning Committee of the Much-Binding-In-The-Marsh District Council.

(Shot of faded typewritten document)

VOICE OVER *(reads)*: Dear Sir. Although I am in fact an extremely important Cabinet Minister, I am writing to you in my capacity as just an ordinary obscure citizen and personal friend of Mrs Thatcher. I am told that Snodgrass Developments Ltd have a plan to erect four dwelling units in my back yard. This is a simply intolerable demand by Snodgrass Developments which will be met with a wall of blood and steel. Of course you are free to make any decision you like with regard to this one, but if you have the barefaced effrontery to approve these applications then I shall have no hesitation in invading Czechoslovakia. Heil Thatchler!

(Shot of signature, which reads "Oberkommandant Kurt Ridlheim, Environmentalisches Sekretariat OKW")

VOICE OVER: We asked Dr Ridlheim whether he could remember writing this letter.

RIDLERTROPP: I have no memory of seeing zis document. It is a blatant forgery. A team of international historians has already shown zat I am innocent as hell, do you understand?

GRITTY VOICE: But did you write this letter, Mr Ridley?

RIMMLER: Zis interview is terminated. Get out of mein agreeable house immediately. I didn't come to live here in the country just to have journalists pushing their way into mein drawing room, und speculators putting hundreds of their dreadful little concrete boxes in mein garden.

THATCHER: You're fired.

VOICE: So, was he guilty or wasn't he? Perhaps we shall never know.

POETRY CORNER

Lines on the defeat of Michael **Meacher** in the High Court in a libel action against the *Observer*.

So.
Farewell then
Michael Meacher's
Money.

Yes, you have
Lost £200,000.

You said
That you were
Poor and your
Family had
Nothing.

Well, now
It is true.

E.J. Thribb (17½)

"Excuse me. Is this the environment?"

"They'll always change it for you if it fits"

NB

The Martyrdom of St. Marietta

by Deirdre Spart

An extract from her forth-coming book *The Real Tragedy of Cleveland*, Lesbos Books, £2.95.

Higgs — The Nightmare Begins

Once again, predictably, the phallocentric media decided that the victim was to be a woman. And Marietta Higgs was the perfect scapegoat.

This brilliant doctor, who worked round the clock to help the ordinary women of Middlesborough, had cou-rageously exposed men for what they are i.e. child abusers, rapists and psycho-paths.

In her first six months she had personally rescued no less than four million children from the clutches of the male sadists of Cleveland.

But was she thanked for her one-woman crusade? No. The male establishment, i.e. doctors, police, MPs, media, lawyers and judges, all rushed to blacken her name and to defend the perverted practices of Cleveland's child abusers.

First of all Higgs was sub-jected to a total campaign of hysterical vilification by the jackals of the Tory press.

Who stood up for Higgs in those dark days when she was being branded as some kind of obsessive lunatic, when in fact she is a fully qualified doctor with years of clinical training in the detection and treatment of men, er, finally she was totally hounded out of her job and put on a show trial at Leeds Court by a male-dominated judge, i.e. Butler-Sloss, who to-tally predictably found her guilty and sentenced her to be burned at the stake.

This book should be available from all progressive bookshops. But if you have difficulty in obtaining it please write direct to Deirdre Spart, Flat 4, 218 Cathy Massitter House, The Mandela Estate (for-merly Herbert Morrison Gardens), Tufnell Park, London SPA RT1.

Exciting new publishing event!

GNOMA

THE MAGAZINE
FOR THE WOMAN OF NOW

YES, it's here at last! The women's monthly with a difference. We at G N O M A have looked long and hard at what you the *modern* woman want to read in *your* magazine. G N O M A is for you, because you are the woman that you are. And we recognise that. G N O M A knows, like no other magazine, the sort of woman who is what she is. A woman of the 80s with an eye on the 90s. G N O M A reflects the real you.

YOU ARE:

A career woman who stays at home looking after the kids.

A homemaker who runs a large office.

Between 16 and 60. Or not.

YOU LOVE:
- *Cooking* ■ *Sewing* ■ *Windsurfing*

YOU HATE:
- *Sewing* ■ *Windsurfing* ■ *Cooking*

YOU are a contradiction, an enigma, someone we know nothing about except that you have a lot of disposable income in your handbag. G N O M A wants *you* to give it to *us* on a regular basis.

LOOK for G N O M A at your newsagent. It'll be next to all the other ones.

ASK for it by name because it'll look like them too.

GNOMA

In this week's debut issue

SEX: Where has the fun gone?
Tasty BARBECUE Hints from the Freezer.
Summer FASHION: The Mini takes off.
The PASTA Diet: It really works.
Office STRESS: How to cope.
Fergie's BABY: Boy or Girl?

PLUS. . . PLUS. . . PLUS. . .
Your Stars. . . Short Story. . .
Beauty Tips. . . Special Offers. . .
Films. . . TV. . .

◄ SEX
► BARBECUE
◄ FASHION
► PASTA
◄ STRESS
► BABIES

ANOTHER DISMAL
WOMEN'S MAG FULL OF ADS

(Shurely shome mishtake – Ed.)

 FREE Sachet of Hair Conditioner

(Published by the GnomeLeisure Corporation)

Stasso

Genius or Sex Fiend?

"My wife makes the best dumplings ever"

by Pablo Picasso-Huffington

This eagerly awaited biography of one of the 20th century's towering geniuses, Arianna Stassinopoulos, has taken America by storm revealing as it does that the world famous creative master known to millions as "Stasso" was in fact the slave of passions so tempestuous that all men became her sexual victims.

Now read on:

She was at the height of her powers when she met the shy wordsmith Bernado Levini. There was an instant magnetism from the moment they met, a sort of inner attraction, a chemistry of the soul so powerful that Levini was swept off his feet and onto the couch by the hot-blooded Athenian earth mother.

There had been other women in his life but never anything like this. He was dominated utterly by her powerful life force, a cruel passion that destroyed him completely. Within a few weeks his reason had gone. She had even reduced him to believing in her mentor, the mystical so-called sex-guru, the Bhagwham Bamthankyou Maam.

Stasso of course, having sucked Levini dry, dropped him callously for someone socially more acceptable, the Texan millionaire Huffington Puffington III Junior.

Meanwhile her internationally successful masterpiece *Maria Callas: A Portrait of Plagiarism* was acclaimed by the law courts as someone else's work. But even during this so-called "in the Red Period" Stasso still exercised her spell over the hopeless Levini *(continued section 94)*

NEXT WEEK: The conquering Greek giantess eats John Selwyn Gummer for breakfast, lunches with Lord Weidenfeld and has a passionate dinner with Sir Laurens van der Post.

TO THE EDITOR OF THE DAILY TELEGRAPH

From Sir Herbert Gussett (MCC and Saloon Bar).

Sir: Like millions of loyal Englishmen, I have found these recent weeks almost more than flesh and blood can bear. Hardly a day goes past without news of another humiliating defeat being inflicted on our hapless so-called cricketers.

Many different suggestions have been made from all quarters as to how the rot can be stopped and England once again restored to her rightful position as the greatest cricketing nation in the world.

Some have suggested that the entire team should be sacked and eleven new players found who could display a little more guts, initiative, leadership and bulldog grit.

Others have rightly recommended that Mr Peter May should be taken out into the middle at Lord's and shot.

Both these points are worthy of consideration, but I still fear that they would fall short of the results that we are looking for — i.e. England 612-1 dec., West Indies 0 all out and 0 all out (Mr Viv Richards 0).

May I therefore put to your readers the Gussett 10-Point Plan To Save England, which was thrashed out during an all-night "think-in" at the Lamb & Flag last Thursday evening? The plan agreed by myself, my friend Lt. Col. Frobisher and our landlord Mr N. Balon was as follows:

THE PLAN

1. All overseas players to be banned from playing against England in Test Matches.
2. New immigration laws to be passed as a matter of urgency to prevent any overseas cricketers being allowed into this country at any time or for any reason.
3. A special recruitment drive to be launched in South Africa to discover ten more players of the quality of Allan Lamb.
4. A change in the laws to allow the umpires to rule at their discretion that England have won any Test Match, irrespective of the score at the time.
5. Huge swarms of highly-trained killer bees to be sent to the Caribbean on a "search and destroy" mission to wipe out all potential fast bowlers, batsmen, fielders etc in local sides before they get to the "dangerous age" (13).
6. Er. . .
7. 8. 9. 10. That's it.

The meeting broke up at 10.37pm when the local police force (PC Jedediah Parsnip) burst in with a cry of "As part of the drive to rid rural England of late-night hooliganism you are all under arrest."

I remain, Sir, in custody, Your obedient prisoner,

H. GUSSETT,
"A" Wing,
HM Prison Binloonie,
Dorset.

Come off it Mr. Smug

WELL, for crying out loud! Guess who scored nil out of 10 on a quiz which any normal *Sun*-reading moron could have answered with his eyes closed?

Yes, it's old Sir Smugface himself, the snotty-nosed Lord Snooty who is going to tell us what we can and what we can't watch on the telly.

These are the questions we put yesterday to TV's new Mr Clean-Up:

Q. Who is Charlene's granny in *The Morons*?
A. Er, I'm afraid I haven't quite caught up with *The Morons*, but my children tell me it's awfully good.

Q. Who is the mechanic in the garage opposite the Dirty Duck in *The Vegetables*?
A. I'm afraid I don't get home in time for *The Vegetables* – that's the new Australian one with the chap in the garage, isn't it?

Q. Whose catchphrase is "Piss off, the lot of you" in *The Yobboes*?
A. Er, is that the one about the police? I'm not sure we can get that in Somerset.

Q. Which American series has a tough-talking dentist whose catchphrase is "Blow 'em away, Hank"?
A. Er, that sounds vaguely familiar. Is it *The Assholes*?

On every single question, Mr Know-All knew nothing.

Yet the Prime Minister seems to think that this pinstriped and po-faced Lord Smartypants from Little Piddling-in-the-Marsh is the right man to stop Rupert Murdoch pumping round-the-clock filth into the nation's sitting rooms through his exciting new Pornosat Smuttelite TV service.

The *Sun* says, good on you, Rupe.

You keep giving us punters a little bit of what we fancy – and kick old Fogey Foureyes back to the Stone Age where he belongs.

Now turn the page upside-down for the correct answers to that Rees-Mogg TV Quiz.

1. Uncle Wally and social worker Mandy in his potting shed.
2. Sergeant Pillbox in *They Never Came Back*.
3. Dirty Kevin and Rita Raunch (Thames, Tues: 3.15).
4. Patrolman Dan Moosebuger of the Monterey Police Department.
5. Sherpa, Mrs Trelford's trusty Airedale in *Tiny's Tots* (LWT, Sun: 5.30).

The Gospel according to Margaret

1. And lo, Maggie came unto the town of Edin-burgh, which is called Auld Ree-kie.
2. And there were gathered together the scribes and moderators of the Church of Scotland.
3. And Maggie opened her mouth and spake, saying:
4. "Blessed are the wealthmakers, for they shall make wealth.
5. "Blessed are they that hunger and thirst after money, for they shall obtain huge amounts of it.
6. "Blessed is the Chancellor of the Ex-chequer, for he shall give to them that hath a great deal more.
7. "Blessed are the thrusting young enterprise culture executives, for they shall have breakfast with Kenneth Clark.
8. "Blessed is the Nicholas Ridley, for he shall inherit the Green Belt.
9. "Blessed are the pure in heart, for they shall have Sir William Rees-Mogg to keep them so.
10. "Blessed is Myself, for reasons too obvious to mention."
11. And they were amazed at her teaching.
12. And she further spake a parable:
13. "The Kingdom of Myself is like unto a wise man that hath a thousand million talents.
14. "And he buried some in a building society account, some in shares in an privatised industry, and the balance in Dockland development schemes.
15. "And there was a foolish man who hath only a small portfolio which was not spread widely.
16. "And then cometh the Wall Street Crash. And the chill wind bloweth upon the City, and the men in shirt-sleeves caught an cold.
17. "And the foolish man cried aloud, saying: 'Woe is me, for I have gone down the toilet.'
18. But the wise man rejoiceth and taketh his wife to *The Phantom of the Opera* and a meal at the Berni Inn, saying: 'I care not, for I am an hundredfold richer.'
19. And the foolish man casteth himself off from an high place.
20. So I say unto you, it is easier for a rich man to have a good time in my kingdom than for a poor person to buy a packet of Camel from the newsagent."

Here endeth the Lesson

"Oh no! It's packed out in here"

I HAVE recently become the proud owner of a very agreeable house in the country, to which I retreat as often as I can.

I have found my weekends in Somerset a revelation. The contrast with living in London is amazing.

One of the first things you notice in the country is the astonishing silence.

In London you hear nothing but the continual noise of cars, buses, taxis and motorbikes. Often it is deafening. Also in London there are millions of people.

Some way to go yet

But in the country it is a different picture altogether. Here there are very few cars, and not many people. A blessed silence reigns everywhere.

It is astonishing and gives one a tremendous sense of peace − a sense that God is in his heaven and I am in my study tapping out another few hundred thousand words for the *Daily Mail.*

Keep going

I have noticed another astonishing thing about the country. Everywhere there are birds, of many different kinds.

One of the greatest joys of my rural existence has been learning to tell the difference between one kind and another.

Already, after only a few months, I have learned to recognize the friendly little red-breasted robin, hopping merrily from twig to twig in search of his prey, and to distinguish it from the huge cawing buzzard which circles menacingly overhead like some archetypal angel of death.

Half way

For that is the message of the countryside.

·DAVID ACE·

Why oh why are we printing this guff by Paul Johnson ?

by PAUL JOHNSON

Because It's New Year And We Haven't Got Anything Else To Put In.

It is an unceasing cycle of change, of life and death, of birth and decay, as the mighty seasons roll on their eternal round, winter, spring, summer, autumn.

How far away London seems, as I drive through the ancient villages which have stood here since the beginning of time, redolent of the very spirit of English history.

The names alone ring a peal like the bells of their church towers — Auberon St. Waugh, Kington Miles, Peregrine Worsthorne, Marmaduke Hussey, Whittam Smith.

Nearly there

And, above all, what is this strange sound I hear echoing through the proud valleys and forests of the mighty Quantock hills?

'Tis the view-hulloo of the gaily garbed huntsman, as he pursues his bushy-tailed quarry o'er fen and lea.

Since moving to the country I have realised that hunting is a wonderful institution, a kind of mystic ritual which binds together all classes of the community in one sacred bond of fellowship, whether they be honest forelock-tugging peasants trudging along on foot, or rich journalists down from London sitting in their Range Rovers.

There is a tremendous air of expectancy. And then, suddenly, there he is — Reynard himself, with his huge flapping ears and pink tusks, trumpeting his proud message of defiance as the king of the jungle.

I thought to myself, how lucky both he and I were to live in the real world of the Somerset countryside.

"Excuse me, but that's my seat. . ."

THE THINK TANK

A farce in two acts by Harold Pinter

ACT I

The curtain rises on the dining room of a fashionable Holland Park residence. A large bookcase dominates the room and a portrait of a beautiful woman hangs over it. Seated at the table are John, a writer and former QC, now overweight and balding. Penny, his second wife; Lady Antonia, the hostess, an incredibly beautiful and amazingly talented woman; Harold, her husband; Drabble and Holroyd, a dull couple who sit uncomfortably at one end of the table.

LADY ANTONIA: Well, here we all are.

(Pause)

HAROLD: Would you please pass the mustard. . .

HOLROYD: We had mustard once in Clacton.

(Pause)

LADY ANTONIA: I've been thinking.

JOHN. Really? This mustard's awfully good. It reminds me of the mustard we brought back from Tuscany.

PENNY *(slowly)*: I agree with Antonia.

We've got to do something. Us.

HOLROYD: If the intellectuals don't, who will?

LADY ANTONIA: I mean. . . I mean. . . *(Pause)* I admire Mrs Thatcher in many ways. She is a woman, after all.

HAROLD: The bitch.

(Long silence)

DRABBLE: Has anyone been to the sales?

JOHN: Of course. You're right. You are right. We can't leave it to Worsthorne and Co.

HAROLD: Bastards!

JOHN: They've had it their way far too long.

(John pours himself a large glass of champagne)

LADY ANTONIA: That's why we're here, isn't it?

PENNY: We should call ourselves something.

HAROLD: The Bastards.

(Pause)

HOLROYD: How about the Mustard Club? We're as keen as mustard, you could look at it like that.

(All laugh nervously. He selects an olive and eats it menacingly)

DRABBLE: By the way, isn't it wonderful about Michael's advance?

HAROLD: Bastard!

PENNY: But I suppose most of it will go in tax?

HOLROYD: No, actually. Not since the Budget.

(Very long silence indeed as all ponder the implications of this remark)

LADY ANTONIA: Let's meet again and fix a date. We must meet regularly.

(They all take out their diaries, except for Harold)

JOHN: Well, I'm away in August.

PENNY: It's Tuscany again.

HOLROYD: We've got a writers' conference in America, we won't be back this September.

LADY ANTONIA: Well, it's Christmas before we get back from Scotland and then I have to get going on this new book. . .

HAROLD: Bastards!

ACT II

The scene is the same except that no one is there. Phone rings for some time. Then stops.

CURTAIN

At the first and only performance of this play the cast was as follows:

Lady Antonia . . . . . . FELICITY KENDALL
Harold . . . . MICHAEL GAMBON
John . . . . LEO McKERN
Penny . . . . UNA STUBBS
Holroyd . . . . MICHAEL WILLIAMS
Drabble . . . . JUDI DENCH

Produced by Sir Peter Hall
Published by Fabber & Fabber Ltd

"I'm rounding up stray supermarket trolleys"

KING GEORGE Vth MEMORIAL HALL, NEASDEN

Exhibition of original cartoons from the *New Dworker* 1901–1988

The only opportunity in Europe to see the pick of 87 years of cartoons from the world's most sophisticated and amusing weekly periodical.

Cartoons by:

Bazig	Tim
Strich	Ruth Zoob
Sam Solly	James Trebor
Consomme	Conrad Winklepicker
Wal Fiddler	Harry O'Hara
Chas N. Dave	Al Koren
Frank Sonovabichz	Dag Loom
Chuck Wot	Norma Welstead
Perry Stroiker	Franklin Bartoldi
Hal Huck	Michael Heath
O. Flugelman	*(Shome mishtake shurely?)*

Open Tuesday to Wednesday Only (closed Tuesday)

The legendary 1921 Soblo drawing capturing the quintessential humour of the *New Dworker*

"Hi, honey, where's the dog?"

"I shot this morning's minion, Mr 'opkins"

SOCIAL SERVICES APPOINTMENTS

Livingstone Borough Council

Following the recent guidelines issued by the Government with regard to the status of the ethnic Romany travelling community, the Council is pleased to announce that vacancies have now arisen with regard to the following new posts within the Council's Equal Opportunities Department:

- **£25,608-£33,721 p.a. (plus London weighting and dislocation expenses).**

  Head of the newly-formed Ethnic Travelling Community (Ropersons) Welfare and Anti-Discrimination Unit.

  The post is open to all white, middle-class, university-educated *Guardian* readers with no experience of anything at all.

- **£15,812-£21,864 (plus all allowances).**

  Ethnic Travelling Community (Romanies of Differing Sexual Orientation) Gay and Lesbian Counselling Team Leader.

  This job is open to anyone who used to work for the GLC and still has not found a cushy number elsewhere — beard and trainers essential.

- **£47,812-£54,216 (plus house, car, interviews on *Newsnight*).**

  Romany Child Abuse Referral Co-ordinator.

  This post is open to abuse.

Please apply (enclosing CV) to the Chief Personnel Recruitment Liaison Facilitator (Ethnic and Sexual Minority Non-Discrimination Division), Livingstone Borough Council, The Portakabin, Brent, London E39 ZZ6.

"Frankly Michael, I think it's possible to take cosmetic surgery too far"

Anniversary celebrations for long-running 'Beano'

by Our Comic Staff
Sir Geoffrey Howe

MINE'S A DOUBLE BOYS AND GIRLS!

ONE of Britain's longest running institutions, the Tory Party *Beano*, this week celebrated ten years of fun, games and fat profits.

Adored by millions although often criticised for being childish, sexist, racist, violent and "fodder for morons", the Tory *Beano* has nevertheless outlasted all its rivals.

LORD SUITY

Since it started its central characters have remained unchanged notably the ever popular "Denis the Thatcher", whose ridiculous exploits have amused young and old alike.

Some features have been dropped and then revived, most notably "Parky the Dodger" who always manages to land on his feet after the trickiest scrapes.

Another old favourite "Lord Whitelaw and His Pals" has only recently been retired as it was felt his brand of "snooty" moderation had fallen out of favour with today's audience.

DOWNING STREET KIDS

One character who did not make it was "Jonah Moore", the man who seems to put a jinx on anything he touches.

But whatever the future one character will always be at the heart of the *Beano*. For many, "Maggie the Minx" has come to embody all that is worst about this appalling old institution *(shome mishtake shurely? Ed.)*

Hamelin Times

FRIDAY JULY 22 1988   7 GUILDER

"EVERYONE TO BLAME FOR PIPER TRAGEDY" — says Judge

by Our Cleveland Staff
LUNCHTIME O'BUSE

In a report out today, the people of the town of Hamelin were told that they were all responsible for the tragedy that had overtaken hundreds of children who had been forcibly removed from their homes by the mysterious Piper.

"There was a general lack of liaison between departments," says Justice Butler-Schloss-Hoffmeister in her 500-page report. "It would be unfair to blame the Piper for kidnapping the children," she says. "Others must also not bear their share of the responsibility."

She named:

● THE MAYOR, who had called in the Piper to deal with rodent abuse. He had, she said, been ill-advised and insufficiently watchful, although acting throughout with the best of motives.

● HAMELIN Social Services department for allowing the Piper to patrol the streets with his pipe abducting the children from their homes, often in broad daylight. "It ought to have rung warning bells," says the report, "when they saw hundreds of children being led through the streets by an itinerant busker."

ESTHER RATZEN

The report, however, did condemn Mr Robert Browning for his "inflammatory

Artist's impression of the Piper at the height of the controversy.

poem" which contained the unfounded allegation that the children had been led away without their parents' consent from under the noses of the authorities.

"There is not the slightest evidence to support any of Mr Browning's suggestions," concluded the report.

Piper is unrepentant

Breaking his long silence, Dr Marietta Piper told Hamelin Radio that she was "perfectly satisfied" with her performance and that she "would do it all again" if she were given the chance. Looking lean but defiant, the whistle-playing figure at the centre of the controversy infuriated his listeners by maintaining his complete innocence in the affair.

Asked about the whereabouts of the children "taken into care", the Piper declared that he would contest all the writs issued by the protest group HPAPP (Hamelin Parents Against Pied Pipers).

PIEDATRICIAN

Last night the Mayor announced a 600,000 million guilder plan for new safeguards against unlawful public pipe playing in front of children. He said that statistics showed that one in three Hamelin children had been exposed in one form or another to pipe-playing and that it was "the biggest single danger confronting Hamelin society today."

The Winner of the 50p Literary Review Prize for Real Poetry That Rhymes

Editor Abraham Wargs writes:

The judges (myself) had absolutely no hesitation in awarding this absurdly generous prize to Mr Septimus Fogey for his quite brilliant poem, *Oh Isn't Everything Awful?*

It is so refreshing, after reading no modern poetry at all, to come across a poem which is really like the sort of things one used to read at school, instead of this awful muck which passes for poetry nowadays. I mean, you take that T.S. Eliot. I mean, what a load of rubbish. My kid can write better than that [*Miss Daisy Waugh, authoress and columnist*].

There's only one sort of language these modern poets understand. String 'em up. I had that Philip Larkin in the back of the *Literary Review* once.

Winning entry: The Very Rev Septimus Fogey

WINNING ENTRY

by the Very Rev Septimus Fogey, 83½, of Quatrains, Combe Offit, Somerset.

*Oh, isn't everything awful, in this terrible
                                    modern age.
It really puts one into a constant sort
                                    of rage.*

*Everywhere one looks, there are pop
                            stars and DJs,
There are model girls and motor cars
                and this frightful skateboard craze.*

*There are people who make their living
                    by appearing on chat shows,
And other beastly programmes
                    that heaven only knows.*

*Who is there left in England
                    who stands for all that's true?
Yes, Mr Abraham Wargs,
                    I'm talking about YOU.*
(or 'and the Literary Review'. I can't decide which is best. S.F.)

CORRECTION

This paper, like all other newspapers, may have given the impression in the course of the last year that we believed the Chancellor, Mr Nigel Lawson, to be an economic genius whose most recent Budget was a brilliant exercise in financial strategy, showing a fiscal dexterity that made him little short of supernatural.

Articles such as those headed "SuperNige Does It Again", "Loadsaluvlylolly" or "Chancellor Provides Necessary Stimulus for Continuing Prosperity" may have been interpreted as suggesting in some way that Mr Lawson knew what he was doing. It would, we concede, have been possible to conclude from these articles that this paper believed the large tax cuts in the Budget to have been a welcome incentive to the economy.

We now realise that Mr Lawson is a complete incompetent and are pleased to make it clear that he is one of the most dangerous idiots ever allowed to take charge of the nation's economy. We also accept that the tax cuts led to a huge consumer and credit boom, a situation which was perfectly obvious to anyone not employed by a rich, right-wing newspaper proprietor, and that this boom has led directly to a massive balance of payments deficit of the type that we blamed the Americans for having last year.

The disastrous nature of Mr Lawson's hopeless ideas is something that we have been saying all along, although we have unaccountably printed exactly the opposite.

We would like to apologise to the country for any misunderstanding that may have arisen from this, and would further like to express our deep sense of regret at any distress that Mr Lawson may have caused.

ESTABLISHED 1791   No. 10251

*** 50p

OBSERVER

Harrods' boss is "tremendous crook"

EXCLUSIVE by Staff Reporter (Donald Trelford)

THE chairman of Harrods Ltd, Mr Mohammed El Fayed, is a tremendous crook, the *Observer* can reveal.

We have been shown documents which confirm beyond any shadow of doubt that Harrods should have been sold to a rival bidder, the well-respected businessman and newspaper proprietor, Mr Tiny Rowland.

The confidential documents relating to the take-over bid for Harrods show that, far from being a bone fide Egyptian prince and multi-billionaire as he claims, Mr Fayed was in fact born in the notorious red-light district of Port Said, the illegitimate son of a night club belly-dancer Miss Fatima Sheikh-it-al-about.

His real name is in fact not Fayed at all but "Filth", an old Egyptian word meaning "tremendous crook".

From his earliest years the self-styled "Fayed" earned his living by stealing melons from itinerant vendors and selling postcards of a salacious nature to visiting American tourists.

Later he somehow managed to persuade the British government that he was a fitting person to own the most famous and prestigious store in the world, Harrods.

Last night a highly placed source came into my office and told me: "Donald, you will be out on your ear if you do not print a front-page exclusive."

Just think of it. I mean, Harrods. It stands for everything that's made this country great, dunnit?. And now it's owned by a load of smelly, jumped-up Arabs. You know what I think? I think there should be a law that a place like Harrods should only be owned by a bona fide British company, like Von Lonrho (Zimbabwe) Plc of Panama.

"Good morning Mr Sigsworth, I'd like to talk to you about the Bible"

"It's all right, officer - this is a Heritage Murder"

Anti-semitism charge against Eliot "disgraceful" scholar claims

by Our Academic Staff
J. Alfred Prufrock

A leading American scholar, Prof. Hiram Q. Pipesucker, has firmly rebutted the recent claim that T.S. Eliot's poetry was responsible for World War Two.

This charge, which was originally made in the *Jewish Chronicle*, has given rise to one of the fiercest literary controversies of all time.

Professor Pipesucker, of New Dworkin University, has written a *Festschrift* to celebrate the 93rd birthday of leading Eliot scholar Phlebas T. Hackenbusch:

It may seem to the layman that some of Eliot's poetry written in the 1920s may be open to the interpretation that it is motivated by the kind of anti-semitism that was to have such unfortunate consequences in later years.

Let us consider, for instance, the poem *The Epiphany of St Simeon Stylites* (1923). Here we find the following lines:

These filthy Jews
Are really ghastly
To my mind
They should all be strung up
If you ask me
It is the only language they
Understand.

J'avais cet Dreyfus dans
La derriere de mon velo,
une fois
Mensa mensa mensam
Bam, bam, bam
Viva Espana!

When we consider the context of this rich web of allegorical and literary allusion in which Eliot couched one of his finest minor poems, we see that the apparent hostility towards the Jews contained in such phrases as "string 'em up" is no more than a Laforguean mask, a playful counterpoint between the schizoid tendencies implicit in contemporary European culture, where the persona of the author is simultaneously a reflection of some of the more violent undercurrents of opinion which then characterised the bourgeois classes, and at the same time speaking in the fragmented linguistic idiom that is symptomatic of a culture in disintegration.

When we consider Eliot's later work, such as the hauntingly mystical *The Final Solution* (1933) and such lines as "God, I hate the Jews" (contd p. 94)

T.S.Eliot — responsible for World War Two?

"Following our disastrous year we have been taken over by a Japanese company - they're not offering golden handshakes. . ."

Winner attacks Charles

Film director Michael Winner hit out today at Prince Charles for suggesting that there was "too much sort of violence in film and video".

Mr Winner, the makei of such well-known films as *Death Rape, Blood Orgy* and *The Sex Muggers*, said:

"How dare this stuck-up twit who is totally out of touch with modern trends in popular entertainment cast aspersions on our great British film industry?

by Our Royalty Staff
Lady Antonia Holden-Guest

"It is lucky for him that we do not live in an age without my films on video or he would undoubtedly have been led out to the scaffold and beheaded the blade slicing through his neck releasing a gush of warm red blood bespattering the severed arteries that twitched convulsively in the last death throes of agony... *(contd p 94)*.

Fergie's baby talks to Private Eye

IN HER first-ever interview, given exclusively to this magazine, Britain's newest Princess speaks frankly as she has never spoken before about her loves, her hopes, her fears and her views on women priests . . .

World exclusive interview by Sir Alistair Brunette, Lady Antonia Holden-Guest and Sir Hugh Montgomery-Massivesnob.

SIR ARSLIKHAIR: Your Royal Highness we appreciate you finding time in your busy schedule, between feeds, to answer our questions on this, if I may say so, auspicious occasion.

PRINCESS FERGLET: Goo, goo, gurgle.

SIR ARSLIKHAIR: Ha, ha, ha. I see you've certainly inherited your mother's tremendous sense of humour.

LADY ANTONIA: May we turn now to your views on the environment? As you look around London for the first time, do you feel that in a real sense the skyline has been irrevocably ruined by these modern architects?

(Ferglet dribbles and throws up)

LADY ANTONIA: Ha, ha, ha. I see you've inherited your father's salty and down-to-earth approach to life!

SIR HUGE: As a direct descendant of such formidable women rulers as Boadicea, Lucrezia Borgia and Queen Salote of Tonga, does it rankle with you, your Royal Highness, that the male members of your family will take precedence in the succession to the throne, even if they have not yet been born? I am thinking of a scenario in which the fourth son of Prince Harry, the then Duke of Milton Keynes, would automatically sit in a pew in front of you at a Garter Investiture Ceremony, provided of course that the King of Norway is absent.

BABY: Z-z-z-z-z

ALL: Ha, ha, ha, your Majesty — can we please all have our peerages now?

ON OTHER PAGES

In the courts

Before Mr Justice Cocklecarrot. The case of Starkers v Maxwell.

MR DESMOND BROWNNOSE QC: You are, are you not, Sidney Filth, the editor of the *Sunday Nipple*?

MR FILTH: I am.

BROWNNOSE: When you printed this story alleging that Miss Starkers had visited an exorcist to rid her of her pathological lust for the Duke of Edinburgh with the headline "Koo In Royal Black Magic Love Pact", did you have any evidence whatsoever?

FILTH: I had a hunch, Your Honour.

COCKLECARROT: And you usually back your hunch, do you, Mr Filth?

(Hysterical sycophantic laughter led by Mr Brownnose as lawyers start totting up their bills)

BROWNNOSE: It would be hard to imagine, would it not, a more hurtful, damaging and disgusting libel than this?

FILTH: No, it wouldn't. You should see next week's issue.

COCKLECARROT: I cannot understand, Mr Filth. If you have no defence at all why have you come to court?

FILTH: Because Robert Maxwell told me to.

COCKLECARROT: Who is Robert Maxwell?

(Laughter from press benches)

SIR EPHRAIM STARBORGLING (for Mr Maxwell): M'Lud, I have with me a five-million-page affidavit signed by Mr Gorbachev, General Jaruzelski and Mr Joe Haines. . .

COCKLECARROT: Who is Joe Haines?

STARBORGLING: . . . which gives a resume of Mr Maxwell's heroic career as Friend of the Earth, enemy of the Boche and benefactor of the human race. . .

COCKLECARROT: Ah, the fat one who owns the football clubs. This case has gone on long enough. I now invite the jury to arrive at their verdict of guilty and award ridiculous damages to Ms Starkers, whose fragrant and frail form has filled the courtroom with loveliness. (Blows kiss to plaintiff)

USHER: All stand.

(Lawyers add "standing allowance" to their bills. Pocket calculators explode from overheating in assessing huge fees)

Lord Gnome, in conjunction with the Royal Doulton Ceramics Division, is proud and privileged to present readers with a unique commemorative offer.

THE YOBBO DINNER SERVICE

Created by the world's finest Ceramics craftsmen, this exquisite 92-piece porcelain dinner service has already been described by Art Experts as "the most perfect example of its genre in the history of commemorative artefacts" (Professor Wedgwood Bonehead, *Plates & Platemen*, 1988).

Each individually thrown dish has on it the portrait of the Royal Couple especially commissioned from the brush of none other than the very wonderful Royal portrait artist Signor Pietro Annigoni. Their Royal Highnesses are shown posing in their underwear on their honeymoon.

Every item in the Yobbo Dinner Service is finished in pure gold leaf with a mother-of-pearl inlay and a varnish of crushed emeralds. The Royal motto — "Gor Blimey! Do they mean us!" — is picked out in wrought silver on the reverse, along with the manufacturer's stamp of quality and authenticity.

☆ There are only seven sets available of this incredible testament to the most historic and moving wedding of all time.

Not only is the Yobbo Dinner Service an Art Treasure of the very highest order, but it is a valuable heirloom for your children and your children's children.

TO avoid disappointment, send cash immediately (£3 million + p&p) to: Lord Gnome's Tasteful Sid Yobbo Offer, Block C, The Lord Young Business Park, Peterborough.

WARNING: THE SID YOBBO DINNER SERVICE CONTAINS SCENES THAT MAY OFFEND MINORS OR PEOPLE OF A NERVOUS DISPOSITION

HOW THEY ARE RELATED

Egbert the Yob = Eggfrieda the Ghastly

Sir Lancelot Yobbo = Matilda the P.R. woman

Derek Ye Yobb = Mistress Blimey of Hacknie on Ye Marsh

Jamus O'Yobbo = Edna O'Brien

"Whistling Sid Yobb, The Cockney Canary" = Doris ("The Laughing Belle of the Tightrope") Hockney from Hackney

Jack the Yobber = Gertie Knockers

Derek Jacyobbi = Elsie Garnett

Sid Yobbo = Mrs Sid Yobbo

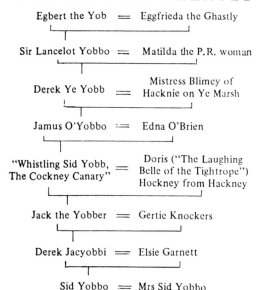

TomJohnston

NEWS AT TEN

(Several minutes of extremely expensive graphics showing London being showered with meteorites which eventually turn into Sir Alastair Burnet's nose)

BONG...

SIR BRUNETTE: Douglas Hurd cracks down on an organisation we cannot name...

BONG...

Millions of Republicans dance in Belfast streets...

BONG...

And we have an exclusive interview with a bearded man whose initials are G.A. which we are not allowed to show you.

SIR SANDWELL GALL: Good evening. The Government today launched an all-out attack on an organisation in Ulster which we cannot name.

(Shot of man in glasses being pushed on to doorstep of No 10 to face microphones)

HURD *(for it is he):* What I am told I have to say to you is that we are absolutely fed up with you-know-who getting all this publicity on the television, and the Prime Minister is absolutely determined that these chaps must never be mentioned again. In the Prime Minister's own phrase, we must cut off the hydrogen bomb of publicity which is the only thing that has been keeping these evil men in the public eye.

(Sound of bomb exploding off-camera. Sir Alastair picks up telephone with concerned look)

BRUNETTE: I am just getting news of a huge explosion in central London. The you-know-who has claimed responsibility. We shall keep you informed of any further developments on this story as this bulletin drones on. Sandy.

GALL: Meanwhile in Belfast old-age terrorists danced openly in the streets hand in hand with men in bala-clavas to celebrate Mrs Thatcher's ban on any mention of the people we are not allowed to mention. At a huge "Victory celebration" a member of parliament with a beard addressed his jubilant supporters.

(Film of man with beard making speech)

VOICE OVER: We are not allowed to show you what this man with a beard is saying, but what he is saying is that he is delighted by the huge propaganda victory handed to him on a plate by the Government and is available to do inter-views with American media teams for the rest of the year. This is a man in a rain-coat in a crowd of people on the Falls Road belonging to that group with the initials — and now back to Sir Gallstone in the studio.

SIR GULLSEGG: In Part Two: more news of the worldwide reaction to the government ban on any further publicity for the chaps with the dark glasses. Plus hundreds of interviews with MPs who are strongly opposed to the Government's clampdown on excessive airtime being given to these fellows with berets. Plus — Bronnie the whale fights for life in a Somerset wine lake.

(CUT TO ADVERT. Ghastly yuppie woman clutching ghastly jar of coffee coyly opens door to admit ghastly smooth man in suit from next door)

WOMAN: Hullo, Cecil, can I help you?

PARKINSON: Yes, Margaret. I want to be Minister of Energy.

MARGARET *(flirtatiously):* But that's just what you are, Cecil. What about some coffee?

PARKINSON: I'm sorry, Prime Minister, I've privatised it.

VOICE OVER: Follow the antics of this ghastly couple tomorrow night at 12.17 (not Neasden or Galashiels). Will they end up in the "Star Chamber" together? That's what the nation wants to know. What are they trying to sell? Everything, silly.

BONG...

BRUNETTE: And now in our special extended bulletin about the need not to give any more publicity to the IRA... whoops!...

(Studio lights go out, to sound of exploding stun grenades, as SAS men storm ITN building shouting "Stop! Police! You have just been shot to stop you using a proscribed set of initials — viz. SAS")

(Continued for several nights running)

(continued from page 94) and after my first marriage broke down I felt that comedy was in a sense... I mean the whole Python experience followed by *Fawlty Towers* was very limiting and..."

He broke off, but some of the old Ministry of Silly Walks magic was still there as he got up and crossed the hotel suite to pour himself a coffee.

"Therapy was a wonderful discovery. If you're English and upper middle class, going into analysis is just a joke. Graham and I used to do sketches about it all the time."

One immediately remembered the classic routines of the Python shows when sketches like the Ministry of Silly Walks became part of the national consciousness.

Looking at him pouring himself a coffee, it is difficult to imagine American audiences now seeing this tall, balding unmistakably English figure as a romantic matinee idol. The Minister of Silly Walks as a sex symbol?

"Well, I thought, if Dudley Moore can do it, why not me?" He laughed, traces of his famous characters Basil Fawlty or the Minister of Silly Walks easily recognisable in that manic grin. He poured himself a coffee.

"Comedy is bloody hard work. I mean, in *Wanda*, which is a fairly complicated story to begin with, Michael, Kevin and Jamie had to... my first marriage... very depressed at the time... giving up comedy... SDP... analysis... book on therapy... Basil... fish... Dudley Moore... hundreds of interviews... same old stuff... you've had your five minutes... next journalist please...

(continued page 95)

GIBRALTAR INQUEST

"We cocked it up" admits mystery voice

by Our Man in Gibraltar
Lunchtime O.

A man describing himself only as "Q" told a crowded coroner's court in Gibraltar today that the killing of three IRA terrorists had been "a terrible mistake" of the type he "would like to make again".

Speaking from behind a 15ft-high concrete wall, specially erected at one end of the courtroom, the witness "Q" was giving evidence on the 94th day of what they are calling "the inquest of the century".

Rocky Horror

Mr Seamus O'Fee, representing the dead IRA terrorists, then cross-examined Mr "Q":

O'FEE: Is it not shameful for a gang of armed men to go around killing people in broad daylight? *(Laughter)*

Q: For me to give an answer to that question would endanger the lives of millions of innocent men, women and children.

SIR EPHRAIM BRIEFCASE QC *(representing the British Government)*: M'Lud, I must intervene at this point to inform the court, if court it be, that I have here a letter from someone whom I am not at liberty to name, for security reasons, but whom I shall merely iden-

tify as Mrs M.T., Supreme Ruler of the Universe.

MR PIZZA-PARLOUR *(Coroner)*: I think I catch your drift, Sir Briefcase. Please get on with your version of the lies.

Rock On Tommy

SIR EPHRAIM: Thank you, Mr Pizzeria. In this letter Mrs Thatcher — whoops, I mean a woman with a name similar to Mrs Thatcher but obviously not her, says that for security reasons this court is not allowed to consider any matters relating to the IRA, Gibraltar, the SAS, or shooting of any kind. But of course any other matter the court wishes to examine is entirely within your province (Northern Ireland). Your witness, Mr O'Fee. Or your fee, Mr O'Witness.

MR O'FEE: What the nationalist community of Ireland want to know is why it was necessary to gun down in cold blood three innocent bona-fide IRA tourists going about their lawful business in a manner only reminiscent of the gruesome and dreadful atrocity in which Padraig O'Marniham was slaughtered by the Block and Tons in Moichael's Bar in Clonakilty in 1912 and does the court not consider that the words of Desmond

O'Ghooley's fine old lament are only too relevant to this present case?

(Sings)

*Under Ben Boolig a young
  Irish lad nestles,
Soon he'll be murdered by
  the bastard B-Specials.*

MR PIZZA-HUT: Silenzio. This is getting out of hand. Call the next witness, Mr Z.

(Enter man with plastic sack over head)

CORONER: Are you Z?

MAN: No, I am H.

CORONER: So you are H?

MAN: No, that is only my code name. My real name is F.

CORONER: I see.

MAN: No. IC is Major D, ie, the last witness.

CORONER: It's all getting very confusing.

ALL: Good.

CORONER: Are there any more letters?

CLERK: No, there's a strike on.

(Laughter. Enter three bearded men disguised as Russian aviators.)

THE MARX BROTHERS *(for it is they)*: We are called O. This one is Chic-O, that one is Harp-O, and I am Grouch-O.

The hearing continues

OLD GRIDIRON

"Ah well, there goes the neighbourhood"

Your American Football Questions answered

Q: I am a Wyoming Wombat fan and I am convinced that, in the 1953 Super Series Play-Off in Nebraska, the Wombat linebacker Jim "Meltdown" McMurtry ran no less than fifteen 30-yard long sacks without conceding a single triple-downer. All that with a broken neck, an injury sustained in the previous week's dramatic 137-136 short-quarter victory over the Oklahoma Geckos!

I say this is a record in an Eastern Pacific Senior Tourney. My nephew Wayne, however, says this record is held by Al "The Avalanche" Alvarez, the legendary yard-skinner of the Illinois Iguanas.

Which of us is right?

Derek Moped,
135 Perry Como Close,
Cricklewood.

Old Gridiron writes: Your query takes me back to that great summer of '29. I was a scout with a little outfit known then as the Seattle Smokies (now, of course, the mighty Moosejaw Meatmincers — no need to fill you in on that gang of quarter stealers!).

Anyway, I just happened in on the fourth half of a pretty middling New York Junior Bears pre-season College goofer and I saw the most amazing looking broad sitting in the front row. Boy! Was she stacked??! Wooo!! Yessirree!

Old Gridiron will be taking a short holiday. Next week: Australian Rules Football with Old Chunder.

A junior doctor writes

Z-z-z-z-z-z-z-z-z-z-z-z-z-z-z-z-z-z-z-z-z-z-z. . .

"Keep back!. . . come near me and I'll destroy the ozone layer!"

POETRY CORNER

Lines On The Imminent Closure Of *The Post* Newspaper:

So. Farewell then
The Post. Brainchild of
Eddie Shah.

"We've got it right this time."
That is your catchphrase.

"We're closing down now."
That is another.

Eddie J. Thribb (17½)

Pensioner's shock advice to Mrs Currie

by Our D.O.S.S. Staff
Doss McWhirter

AT A press conference given last night at the Fred Mulley Eventide Retirement Home, Solihull, senior citizen Mrs Enid Drains offered some startling advice to Britain's outspoken junior health minister, Mrs Edliner Currie.

"My advice to Mrs Currie," she said, "is very simple. She should spend the winter evenings knitting herself some long woollen socks and she should then open her mouth and put a sock in it.

"That would give all the old-age pensioners of Britain a really warm feeling that would last us until the spring."

Edwina Currie is 24.

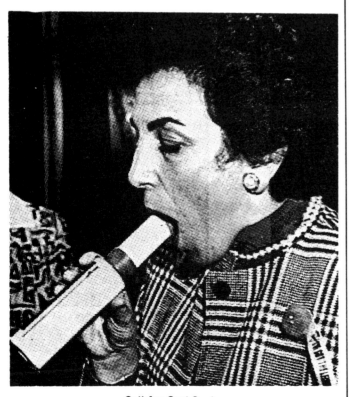

Call for Oral Socks

ANDY LASHES ESTHER

by Our Royal Staff
James Makeitup

An outraged Duke of York today hit out at Dame Esther Rantzen for "heartlessly leaving her brains at home when she went out to work".

"What a hard woman she is," said the controversial Prince. "Every day she goes to her office at the BBC but her little brains are left behind. It is a scandal. There should be a programme about it on BBC1."

Later a spokesman for the Prince said he had been the victim of a cruel misprint. He had meant to say "bairns" not "brains", implying that Esther was a hypocrite and not that she was merely stupid.

Maggie says "Make Love, not War" shock

by Lunchtime O'Flower-Power

In her most amazing about-turn yet, the Prime Minister, Mrs Margaret Thatcher (to be known henceforth to her millions of followers as Shri Maharagie Greenpeace), announced that what the country needed was "a reappraisal of our inner Karma".

Karma Chameleon

Dressed in her new outfit of full-length Afghan coat, and wearing flowers in her perm, Britain's spiritual leader explained some of her new theories to an astonished meeting of the Adam Smith Institute (the right-wing policy group).

After an hour of silent meditation, in which Shri Maharagie sat in the lotus position, the Reincarnated Holy One gave the amazed Conservative assembly a mantra that summarised the new age: "Peace and love, yin and yang, John and Yoko!" they chanted.

Sir Keith Joseph and his Amazing Technicolour Dream Coat

Following the chanting of the mantra, the former Conservative hardliner made it clear that her government was going to look long and hard at the pressing issues of the day — ie, free love, brown rice, and the immediate withdrawal of troops from Vietnam.

"People should do their own thing," she said. "Like, you know, Tune In, Switch Off and Vote Tory."

Mrs Thatcher is desperate.

SPRING BOOKS

A selection by our Literary Editor of the most ridiculous books published this week.

Extremely Rich
by Richard Burton

The heartrending, ultimately tragic story of the humble working class boy from the valleys of Cumbria who discovers a gift for words that turns him into a world megastar. Soon his unmistakable adenoidal tones and craggy sex appeal rocket him to the dizzy heights of the *South Bank Show*. But, like the hero of a Greek tragedy, he is unable to cope with his destiny. His decline makes sad reading, until in the final chapter we see him, a broken shadow of his former self, reduced to interviewing Ned Twinky on *Start the Week*.

Why Young is a Bastard
by Norman Tebbit

At last, in this outspoken 785-page autobiography, one of the greatest statesmen of our age reveals one of the best-kept secrets of the war — ie, that Lord Young of Suit is a tremendous bastard, whose greatest blunder was to oust Normo Tebbs from the No 1 slot as Maggie's top toady *(Shurely Tory? Ed).*

The Why Oh Why Book of Intellectuals
by Paul Johnson

World-famous historian Johnson asks why it is that all the leading intellectuals who have shaped our age are totally discredited by their appalling private lives. Although happy to pontificate on great moral issues, they are very often pitifully inadequate human beings, prey to drink and writing for the *Daily Mail*.

Thatch says "Come off it Hitler"

❝ Monsieur Delorean, mesdames, messieurs. Don't get me wrong, I've got nothing against Europe or the people who live there. We share a common culture. Most of you speak English. You watch many of our fine television programmes, such as *Dallas, Dynasty* and *'Allo, 'Allo*. Many of you will have visited with pleasure our great cathedrals, our Stonehenge, our Stratford-on-Avon, our lions of Longleat. You have seen our great Ian Botham wandering with his elephant Maxwell through the streets of your tiny villages. You have welcomed our soccer hooligans with open gaols. In short, you do not need to tell me how much Britain has meant to all of you, as we have battled to defend you over the centuries against the vicious attacks of the Germans, the Italians, the French, and the ever-threatening Swiss. So there is no need to lecture me on what it means to be a European. I'm British and I recognise that we did not beat you all in two World Wars just to be bossed around by a load of faceless bureaucrats in Brussels. When it comes to faceless bureaucrats, we in Britain lead the world. It would be hard to find a more faceless bureaucrat than my old friend Lord Young of Suit. So the message is clear to all you foreigners. We will fight you on the beaches, we will fight you in the streets, we will never surrender. The Falklands are part of Europe and always have been. Those of us who lived to see this day shall stand on tip-toe when we hear the name of St Crispin. Once more unto the beach, dear friends, where we shall fight them... Oh, have I said that bit before? **❞**

(Enter Hologram of Lord Olivier in the role of Winston Churchill, hovering over the head of St Joan of Thatch, as the massed synthesisers of M. Jean-Michel Jarre strike up Land of Hope and Glory *and giant red, white and blue lasers spell out the message "Vote Conservative".)*

(That's enough speech — Ed.)

CHANNEL FOUR

THAT REES-MOGG SEX SHOCKER IN FULL

YOUNG LADY PRESENTER *(reading not very well from autocue):* Sex on television. When television in this country is deregulated, our airwaves will suddenly be flooded with this type of material which some viewers may find worth turning on their videos for to look at later.

(Shot of mini-skirted French model taking off clothes and pouting to camera. Caption: "Bonjour, Mademoiselle Sexy — Channel No 5 on RTF7")

PRESENTER: Or how about this popular Italian housewife strip quiz show — *Buongiorno Signorina Sexy* from the Torino-based cable service Fiat Uno?

(Shot of sultry Italian temptress cooking spaghetti with no clothes on)

PRESENTER: Or could our living rooms be invaded by this sort of scene from *Guten Morgen Fraulein Sexy,* a nightly soap shown by Dusseldorf Direkt, set in a Black Forest nudist camp?

(Shot of two bare-breasted blonde German ladies wrestling in the snow)

MICHAEL COCK: Tonight, as we continue our in-depth attempt to get anyone to watch our exciting new Channel Four arts programme, we have searched through the archives to find some sex on British television in the past, and this is what we've come up with. In 1958 this scene caused a nationwide storm:

(Clip of Anna Neagle wearing off-the-shoulder dress in TV adaptation of Tulips On Broadway*)*

COCK: Even then, the prudes and killjoys were up in arms at what they considered to be a full-frontal assault on family life. But five years later worse was to come, as Ned Twinky, the inventor of TV satire, recalls.

(Cut to fat man looking smug)

TWINKY: I think all of us can remember exactly where we were on that historic night in 1965 when we saw Kenneth Tynan being the first person in the history of the world to use "that word" on television. It is a tragedy that no footage has survived of the actual moment when Ken said "Fuck". None of us in the studio at the time thought that anything unusual had happened, but the following morning all hell broke loose.

(Cut to newspaper headlines of the time reading "That Word — A Nation's Shame", "MPs Demand Death Penalty For Four-Letter Man", Audience starts to get bored and begins switching channels in the hope of finding some sex on News At Ten. *They discover Alastair Burnet announcing the Israeli election results and switch back to Channel Four-Play)*

COCK: But even this was to pale into insignificance compared with this scene from Dennis Plodder's award-winning 1968 Wednesday Play *The Angel and Mrs Fothergill.*

(Clip of sexy nurse taking her clothes off in a church while the vicar in the pulpit mimes to old recording of Jack Hylton's Band playing Swingtime in Old Alabamy*)*

VICAR: Oh, golly, I must concentrate on something really boring — like a play by Dennis Plodder, or an interview with Dennis Plodder. . .

(Cut to 1973 interview with the whingeing playwright)

PLODDER: All my plays are intensely personal — I'm the only one who enjoys them. Those bastards at the BBC are always trying to put me down by showering me with money and putting on my plays at peak time, the bastards.

COCK: But now, after years of pressure from Mrs Whitehouse to stop viewers seeing the sort of programmes they want, Mrs Thatchouse has set up a powerful new body, the British Sex Council, to ensure that scenes like this will never again be seen on British television:

(Clip from 1975 classic Danish Dentist On The Job *showing pretty, curvaceous blonde dental assistant unzipping trousers of man in chair. Children in pyjamas rush down to join parents in front of screen)*

COCK: We confronted Lord Really-Smugg, the chairman of No Sex Please — We're British, and asked him what right he thought he had to tell us what to watch.

(Cut to agreeable-looking antiquarian bookseller in Somerset rectory study. Caption: "TV's Mr Sexy")

LORD SMUGG *(for it is he):* I don't anticipate that we shall have any real problem with programmes on, for instance, the return to the Gold Standard. But we enter something of a grey area when it comes to any sort of. . . er. . . um. . . you know. . . more of an. . . well. . .

COCK: You mean full-frontal bonking?

SMUGG: Er. . . yes. . . well. . . I didn't quite say that. I was thinking more of. . .

(Children go back to bed. Fathers go to fridge to see if there's any lager left)

COCK: So, if Lord Smugg and the censors have their way, it won't be long before we're never allowed to make programmes like this — ie lots of waffle with a few tits and bums to cheer it up — ever again. In Part Two, we ask if the British public is ready to see other members of the public talking openly on screen about whether Lord Smugg is right.

© *Cock Films, Filth Street, Soho, 1988 — "Let us video your wedding night".*

Yes! It's boozing bonking Britain!

by our Survey Staff

OVER 98% of people in the country had sexual intercourse in the last two hours, according to government statistics published today.

Potato crisps remain the staple diet of the average Mr and Mrs Britain who will spend at least 48 hours a day watching television.

Ownership of CD players has reached a record 1% of the population but to date there are few signs of an end to the north/south divide.

People in the Midlands still get up four hours earlier than people in the south because it is still dark. 74% of all families north of the Wash have no inside Jacuzzi facilities yet they are more likely than their southern counterparts to own their own gerbil.

In Scotland, on the other hand, at least 93% of people are homosexual or enjoy a stable relationship with someone other than their mother.

de la Nougerede

"Good Heavens, Robson - SILLY CONE VALLEY!"

HEALTH EDUCATION AUTHORITY

A I D S

C H A R T E R

WE, the undersigned, are all extremely famous and important.

It is a matter of the utmost urgency that all people who are not as famous and important as we are should listen to what we have to say.

When ordinary people see the most important and famous names in the country at the bottom of this advertisement they will be terrifically impressed and say: "Gosh, aren't those people tremendously famous and important?"

That is why we appeal to everyone to read our names and remember them.

DAVID ABBOTT	BARRY FANTONI	NED SHERRIN
PROFESSOR M W ADLER	DR CHARLES FARTHING	CATHY SHIPTON
SOPHIE ALDRED	EVE FERRET	CLARE SHORT
LINDSAY ANDERSON	MICHAEL FISH	CARMEN SILVERA
PROFESSOR R M ANDERSON	BRYAN FORBES	SUE SLIPMAN
PADDY ASHDOWN	CLARE FRANCIS	SIR GEORG SOLTI
JACK ASHLEY	LADY ANTONIA FRASER	JIMMY SOMERVILLE
RICK ASTLEY	DAWN FRENCH	STEPHEN SPENDER
LORD ASTOR OF HEVER	SIR CLEMENT FREUD	THE RT HON DAVID STEEL
CORAL ATKINS	EMMA FREUD	DR MIRIAM STOPPARD
ROWAN ATKINSON	STEPHEN FRY	UNA STUBBS
RICHARD ATTENBOROUGH	FIONA FULLERTON	JANET SUZMAN
ALAN AYCKBOURN	PAUL GAMBACCINI	GRAHAM TAYLOR
BERYL BAINBRIDGE	DR GRAEME GARDEN	ALICE THOMAS ELLIS
JOAN BAKEWELL		RT REV JAMES THOMPSON
JOHN BANHAM		SOPHIE WARD
THELMA BARLOW		RUBY WAX
BIDDY BAXTER		(CONT. P.94)

WORLD AIDS DAY DEC 1, 1988 JOIN THE WORLDWIDE EFFORT

Issued by Mrs Edwina Currie in the interests of wasting money.

SK-EYE

TELEVISION

THE RIGHT CHOICE

THE COUNTDOWN BEGINS

by Our Media Staff
Mr R. Murdoch

IN AN unprecedented scoop we can reveal that SK-EYE TV has entered into a multi-million-pound deal with one of the world's most talented entertainers, Mr Sid Yobbo, or Old Yel as he is known.

Sid, the most loved figure in Britain, will present a round-the-clock, five-times-an-hour chat show with international celebrities like Andrew Neil (Old Nel), Frank Bough (Old Bel) and Rupert Murdoch (Foul Smell) *(Shurely "Old Mel"? Ed.)*

Bob-a-Yob

Said a jubilant Sid: "Wogan never had nuffink like this. Eat your heart out, Tel! Fancy Old Sel coming down to you from outer space. Blimey! What would my old granny (Old Grel) have thought if she could have lived to see her tiny Del becoming the most important man in the galaxy!"

Taking time off from conducting the London Symphony Orchestra in a recording of *The Sid Yobbo Classical Smashers Collection*, SK-EYE's super new signing went on to describe his early years living in a matchbox in London's East End.

"Those were 'ard days. We lived off whelks and skates' eyes. There was a lot of love about but none of it near me, unfortunately," he said.

Did the darling of the housewives mind being called "Derek Jameson", the cruel nickname given him by the so-called satire magazine *Private Eye*? As tears welled up in his ears, he confessed: "It hurts, but I've learned to live with it as indeed will the rest of the world's viewers."

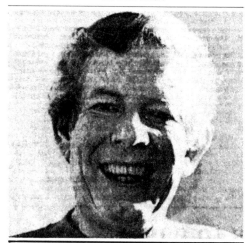

What you will see in 94 days' time
EXCLUSIVE!

Big First-Run Films, including:

Ten Danced In Naples *(MGM)*
They Flew To Bruges *(Repeat)*
One Of Our Baboons Is Missing *(Disney)*
Nightmare Of The Living Eel *(Warner)*
Swedish Dentist Goes Bonking Mad *(Scandoporn)*

PLUS

Up-to-the-minute news from the *Sun* Insight Team and the *Sunday Times* Newsfax Service presented by Simon Dee and Samantha Fox.

(That's enough SK-EYE TV — Ed)
(No it isn't — R.M.)

SK-EYE LINES

Bonking Boffo to join Yobbo

ANOTHER top TV megastar, Frank Bonk (Old Frel) is to join SK-EYE's dazzling line-up of dead-beats and old bores *(Shurely "megastars"? Ed)*.

Old Bel, famed for his cuddly sweaters and coke-sniffing, is no stranger, however, to the "highlife".

"Now I really am spaced out," quipped the balding ex-Breakfast TV heartthrob.

Did he regret his fall from grace at the Beeb?

"We all make mistakes," he said, "and this looks like another one."

Dirty Disher

FOR AS little as £8 now and £300 a month for the rest of your life, you too can receive SK-EYE TV's marvellous range of adverts. *(This does not include the Gnome SK-EYE Dish, Linda Lusardi, which comes in easily assembled kit form at a mere £3,300.35p.)*

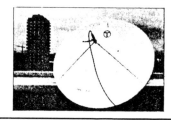

The agony of a typical Thatcher

by Our Man on the Farm, **Old MacGregor**

"IT IS a tragedy. I have lost one of my top birds. She was one of my best liars, sorry, layers. And all at Christmas as well." So spoke a heartbroken Mrs Margaret Hatcher, proprietor of one of the biggest egg-laying governments in the country, who has been forced to destroy Edwina Currie after the public loss of confidence in her.

Fowl

"Apart from myself she was the most dreadful old boiler we had, someone who had repeatedly delivered batches of biggies for years.

"There is no conclusive proof that Edwina is poisonous, though I think she is. One minute she was squawking away, telling old people to knit their own central heating, the next minute I had to put her down."

At this point Mrs Thatcher broke down in tears.

"We gave her free range and she thrived on it. But now, because the farmers are up in arms and the health lobby have fed her a load of truth, sorry, rubbish, I've had to wring her neck.

"We are all deeply sorry at this national tragedy."

Sir Richard Body is 97.

SPOT THE DIFFERENCE

In recent days it has become increasingly clear (writes our Middle Eastern expert, a grey man in a suit whose name we can't remember) that a growing gulf is opening up in Iran between the hard-line fanatical fundamentalists and the more moderate pragmatists.

The whole future of the Middle East could depend on the outcome of this power struggle.

THE EXTREMISTS

Ayatollah Khilirushdie, 107. LEADER of the extreme hardline Shi'ite Pan-Islamic People's Revolutionary faction. He believes that Salman Rushdie and everyone who has ever bought a Penguin book should be publicly disembowelled, and that all their relatives should be burned slowly to death on Iranian television.

THE MODERATES

Ayatollah Rushdiekillie, 108. LEADER of the moderate Shi'ite Pan-Islamic Revolutionary People's faction. He would prefer to see some type of compromise solution to the Rushdie problem, involving the cutting of Mr Rushdie into small pieces and the release of huge clouds of deadly mustard gas over the British Isles as "a heavenly punishment" of the British people for allowing Mr Rushdie's book to be published.

"Excuse me, is this Alcoholics Hieronymous?"

A Camel Driver writes

Every week a well known camel driver is invited to condemn someone to death. This week:

Abdul Al-Haqney *(Camel No. 376)* **on "The Satanic Verses"**

'E's got a nerve that Rushdie blasphemin' and that. 'Ow would he like it if we went round insultin' what he believes in? I tell you, guv, I haven't read the book myself but the Ayatollah's got it right. It makes me mad. You know what I'd do? String 'im up. It's the only language he understands.

I 'ad that T.E. Lawrence in the back of the cab once.

Thousands of books destroyed in new health scare

by Our Literary Staff
Dr Jonathon Mullah

The multi-million pound book industry (W.H.Smug) tonight caved in under pressure from health-conscious Muslims and withdrew thousands of copies of books entitled *The Satanic Verses*.

This followed claims that these books were infected by Salmonella Rushdie, a particularly mild strain of anti-Muslim writing, or AMW as it is known.

CHICKEN

Said W.H.Smug Chairman, Sir John Spineless: "We know perfectly well that there is nothing the matter with these products. They are quite harmless and ordinary people are not in any way affected by them."

"However, there are some people who it is possible may suffer from Salmonella Rushdie and the symptoms can be quite serious. Their eyes widen, they start screaming foreign rubbish and they try and set fire to everything."

YELLOW

He continued, "W.H.Smug are champions of an author's right to say what he thinks. We believe in freedom of speech. However, we also believe in avoiding trouble at all costs, that is why we are removing this particularly offensive book on a temporary ten year basis to allow tempers to cool down. It will be replaced by copies of the very wonderful *Koran*."

Alan Koran is 71.

LETTERS TO THE EDITOR

From Mr Doald Duck
Sir, I support utterly the sacred principle of freedom of expression, for which millions have given their lives in several world wars, and which is the absolute cornerstone of our democratic way of life.
However, it is quite plain to me that this Rushdie chap is just hoping to cash in with a vulgar publicity stunt, designed merely to turn his worthless, tasteless, squalid and deeply offensive little book into a lucrative best-seller. What a shameless self-publicist I am.
Yours faithfully,
ROALD DAHL,
c/o Dahl Promotions plc,
The Chocolate Factory,
Tring, Beds.

From The Chief Rabbi
Sir, I support utterly the sacred principle of free speech, for which millions have given their lives in several world wars and which is the absolute cornerstone of our democratic way of life.

However, the religious sensibilities of other creeds must at all times be respected. Individual freedoms must always go hand in hand with a deep sense of responsibility. That is why this Rushdie chap should be strung up as a salutary lesson to anyone who may be tempted to have a go at me and my lot.
Yours faithfully,
THE CHIEF RABBIT,
Watership Down, Berks.

From Mr Gerald Kaufperson and many other worried MPs
Sir, We support utterly the sacred principle of free speech, for which millions have given their lives in several world wars, and which is the absolute cornerstone of our democratic way of life.
However, in our constituencies there are many Moslems who are deeply offended by MPs who do not stand up to demand the total banning of The Satanic Verses and the public enstringment of its author, and it is

quite possible that if we do not write this letter they will vote for someone else.
Yours faithfully,
G.K. AUFFMANand others,
In hiding, somewhere in Northern England.

From The Chairman of British Consolidated Thumbscrews plc
Sir, I support utterly the sacred principle of free speech, for which millions have given their lives in several world wars, and which is the absolute cornerstone of our democratic way of life.
However, this country has many traditional cultural and economic links with the great people of Iran and it would be the sheerest folly to allow these to be thrown lightly into jeopardy.
My company recently concluded a deal with the Iranian Secret Police which would have brought in to this country millions of pounds' worth of much-needed export business. Now all this has been thrown away by

the criminal folly of allowing the publication of some stupid book by an author who deserves to be shot.
Yours faithfully,
P.W.B. HIMMLER,
The British Rack Corporation,
Trelford New Town, W. Midlands.

From The Chairman of Penguin Books plc
Sir, I support utterly the sacred principle of free speech, for which millions have given their lives in several world wars, and which is the absolute cornerstone of our democratic way of life.
However, in view of the widespread distress which has been caused to the Moslem community throughout the world by the publication of *The Satanic Verses*, we believe that very serious consideration should be given to banning this book as soon as possible.
Yours faithfully,
NAME AND ADDRESS SUPPLIED.

"Thank goodness she's got domestic science to fall back on"

Lines on the Historic Occasion of the Official Dinner given in The White House to say Farewell to President Reagan

Composed by Mr. William McGonagall

'Twas in the month of November in 1988
　That the great President Reagan decided to
　　　　celebrate.
For he knew that he would have to retire in 1989,
　And that is why he invited Mrs Thatcher over
　　　　to dine.

It would be hard to imagine a more glittering scene,
　Unless the occasion had been graced by Her
　　　　Majesty The Queen.
The great ones of the nation stood patiently in line
　To toast their beloved President in Californian
　　　　wine.

O! What a host of geniuses had assembled together,
　Led by the greatest composer in the world,
　　　　Andrew Lloyd Webber,
And also the great novelist, seated on Mrs Reagan's
　　　　right,
　Mr Thomas Wolfe, in his famous suit so white.

And, fresh from his much-acclaimed retrospective
　　　　at the Tate,
　Came Mr David Hockney, with a small blond
　　　　mate.
The preacher Billy Graham did not know what to
　　　　say,
　He had never before been sat at dinner with a gay.

There then fell on the company a mighty hush
　As there entered the President Elect, George
　　　　Bush.
But the President's staff had neglected to mail
　An invitation to the Vice-President Elect,
　　　　J. Danforth Quayle.

Finally the lights dimmed at the climax of the ball
　For the entrance of the most glittering guest of all.
When it came to glamour there was no one to match
　The radiant figure of Mrs Margaret Thatch.

A mighty cheer rose up from the throng.
　It was what they had been waiting for all along.
The sight of the greatest stateswoman the world
　　　　has known,
　Who specially from Gatwick that morning had
　　　　flown.

As she stood before them in all her glory,
　Everyone present wished they too could have
　　　　voted Tory.
What did it matter that they were losing Ron —
　When the immortal Iron Lady would go on
　　　　and on and on?

© W. McGonagall

"You spoil that piranha fish, Derek!"

"PITCAIRN NOT A PUSHOVER"

ROBSON'S SHOCK WARNING

by **I.D. Card**, Our Man Caught In The Turnstiles With The Salmonella-Flavoured Egg Sandwiches And A Copy Of The *Literary Review*.

A defiant Bobby Robson last night warned England fans not to expect an easy passage in next month's first leg of the Group Z zonal World Cup qualifying round when the England squad faces the unknown Pitcairn Island team.

Said Robson: "In football nothing is a certainty. There is no such thing as an easy match in the world of soccer today, particularly for the teams I pick.

Sick as a Poirot

"Remember, when you're talking of Pitcairn you're talking of a team that drew 1-1 with Belize last month and who were desperately unlucky to lose 7-nil to a much-improved Lanzarote.

"They may all be part-timers, these Pitcairn lads, but they've got three first-class players in the Christian brothers (Steve, Gary and Gauguin) and once they've found another eight they'll be a very difficult team to play — especially at football, which is not our strong suit.

"We shall not be naming our team until after the game." Bobby Robson is 59.

LATE SCORE

England 0   Nagorno-Karabakh 12

Unknown man gained access to cabinet

By Our Aeroplane Staff
Edward Heathrow

A member of the public was yesterday revealed to have infiltrated No 10 Downing Street and been given a job as a Transport Minister.

Mr Paul Channon, of no fixed opinions, claimed that he had simply walked in dressed as an Old Etonian and had immediately been appointed a senior minister despite the fact that he had no valid credentials at all.

"I know nothing about transport, let alone airport safety, which I was expected to deal with," he admitted. "I could not believe it. I was given free run of the House of Commons and I even at one stage spoke to the Prime Minister."

A-Paul-ing

When she was told, Mrs Thatcher was said to be livid at this latest failure to screen people trying to penetrate Cabinet security.

Over the last ten years several hundred complete deadbeats have been given jobs without any proper checks being made.

Cecil Parkinson is 57

PRESIDENT BUSH
AN APOLOGY

IN recent months, in common with all other newspapers on both sides of the Atlantic, we may have given the impression that we considered Mr George Bush to be a "hopeless nonentity" and "a wimp with as much charisma as a plastic paper-clip on a wet Friday afternoon in Cincinnati".

We now accept that there was not a scintilla of truth in these totally unwarranted and unfounded allegations. We recognise that President Bush is in fact a statesman of towering stature, with an unequalled grasp of all aspects of foreign and domestic politics.

He is, furthermore, an immensely dynamic, vigorous, punchy, tough, big-shouldered, stetson-wearing, cowboy boots, deep-sea fishing, Ernest Hemingway, John Wayne, real hunk of manhood, yes sirree, richer 'n six foot up a bull's ass, go on punk, make my day kinda guy.

We would now like to take this opportunity to put on record our sincere apologies to President Butch for any misunderstanding that may inadvertently have occurred.

ROSES ARE RED
VIOLETS ARE BLUE
PLEASE SPARE A PENNY
FOR A STARVING POET.

The Literary Event of the Century

For years it has been known by scholars that there existed a priceless hoard of intimate letters penned by the greatest poet of the twentieth century, Clive James (*Shurely T.S. Eliot? Ed*).

Now at last Lord Gnome, in conjunction with Fabber & Fabber, has acquired exclusive rights to market T.S. Eliot t-shirts, car stickers bearing the legend "We Have Seen the Cats of Lloyd Webber", and mugs emblazoned with the motif "I Love J. Alfred Prufrock". Given away free with each mug will be a copy of the book they are calling *The T.S. Eliot Letters*.

Already acclaimed by critics, even before they have read them, these letters give a unique insight into the literary history of the 20th century, and also into the prolonged personal anguish which this towering genius endured in order to produce the first volume of his long-awaited biography of George Bernard Levin (*Shurely sheveral mishtakes? Ed*).

Now read on:

In 1923, when Eliot was 33, he took a job in the Servicetill Department of the National Westminster Bank.

The glittering literary world of London in the 20s (Eliot not in picture)

June 30th, 1927

Dear Mother,
    What wonderful news! I have just been offered a job in the Servicetill Department of the National Westminster Bank. The pay is only 7/6d a week – that is about a dollar and 30 cents – but who knows where it may lead? One day I might even rise to be a Branch Manager, which is I know what you have always wanted for me.
                    Your affectionate son,
                    T.S. Eliot.

PS: I have just written a poem called The Waste Paper Basket. My friend Ezra says the title will never catch on. I may change it. Please send some money and the blue leather gloves under the baseball bat in the bottom drawer in my room. I do not want the baseball bat.

July 14th, 1927

Dear Mother,
    Thank you very much for the gloves, which arrived safely, and also for the cough lozenges. You shouldn't have bothered to send the baseball bat, but I'm sure I'll find some use for it.
                    Your affectionate son,
                    Thomas Stearns Eliot.

PS: Please send more money. By the way, I have changed the title of The Waste Paper Basket to The Baseball Bat. My friend Ezra says it is an improvement, but still not right. Please send more money – oh, I may have mentioned that already!

To Ezra Pound:

August 14th.

Il Tagliatelli Maestro,
*   Hi, O mighty sage,*
*   You'd never guess my weekly wage*
*   Hath risen to a princely pound,*
*   A ref. to your good self,*
*   I will be bound!*
*   Have done more work on The Baseball*
Bat and enclose new sections entitled
Phoenician Filling Station, The Ramayana
Backgammon, and Tutsi-Frutsi Ice Cream.
*   As you will see, the last includes a*
version of the entire New Testament
translated into Cockney rhyming slang.
Do you think I've overdone it?
*   Let me know soonest, O Carbonaro*
Magnifico, what advance you think I can
ask for. £10?
*   Your 'umble servant,*
*   T.S. Eliot (Poet).*

A rare photograph of George Eliot

To the Editor of the Daily Telegraph:

August 30th, 1927

Dear Sir,
*   Your editorial on the need to uphold*
the Gold Standard strikes a welcome note
of realism. As someone who is employed,
albeit in a humble capacity, in the banking
community, I would just like to add that
in my view the fluctuating exchange rate
can only lead to the disintegration of
modern civilisation.
*   Yr humble & obedient*
*   servant,*
*   T.S. Eliot.*

PS: I have written a poem on this subject
called The Baseball Vat, which you might
like to publish for a small consideration.
Shall we say £10?

[Editor's Note: This letter was never published
– see below]

Dear Sir,
*   The Editor thanks you for your com-*
munication of the 30th August, which he
has read with great interest. Owing to
pressure on space, however, he is unable
to print it.
*   Yours faithfully,*
*   L. Gidding.*

Tuesday

Dear Ethel,
*   Thank you for the sugar you lent me*
last week, and for the loan of £1. I am
returning the sugar with this note.
*   Unfortunately I will not be able to*
come and read to you tomorrow, as I
have to take our cat to the vet. Vivien
thinks he has slipped a disc.
*   Yours ever,*
*   TSE.*

PS: Could you see your way to advancing
me a little something extra to go towards
the vet's bill? I would be most awfully
grateful.

PPS: I am thinking of calling my new
poem The Baseball Cat.

From Mr E.M. Stebbings FRVS
To Mr and Mrs T. Eliot:

Dear Sir/Madam,
*   We note with regret that your*
account for veterinary services re Tiddles
the cat has now been outstanding since
1924. Please remit 14/7d without delay.
*   Yours,*
*   Stebbings.*

September 30th, 1927

Dear Stebbings (or should I say
"Stebbingstein"?),
*   You rascally Jew, masquerading as a*
Britisher! You're all the same under your
stones, with your cigars and your
Baedekers. I am thinking of writing a
poem about you.
*   Yours,*
*   T.S. Eliot.*

PS: Would you accept in payment of
your bill the manuscript of a poem I have
written called The Baseball Vet? One day
it could be worth something.

TOMORROW: Mrs Eliot goes to the dentist, and T.S. Eliot changes the name of The Baseball Vet back to his original idea of The NatWest Land.   © *Il Miglior Faber 1988.*

Capitalist Bastard, Capitalist Bastard. . ."

IN THE COURTS

Mr Elton John vs The Sun Newspaper
Settlement Agreed

The Winner

The Winner

SIR EPHRAIM STARBORG-LING *(on behalf of the Sun):* M'Lud, I appear very briefly and pick up a huge cheque acting on behalf of Mr Rupert Murdoch, commonly known as the Dirty Digger, and the *Sun* newspaper.

The *Sun* reported that Mr John, a popular singer, had on a specific occasion engaged in un-mentionable acts with minors, domestic pets and household appliances.

Under the heading "You Filthy Poof", the newspaper further alleged that Mr John was providing narcotic substances for his guests, who included members of the Royal Family, the Archbishop of Canterbury, and Mr Andreas Whittam-Smith, editor of the *Independent*.

When Mr John issued a writ, my clients printed further statements under the headings "Sod Off Pervy", "Get Lost Gayboy", and "Mr Elton John: An Apology".

The *Sun* now recognises that there was not a word of truth in any of these reports, which were based on reliable information and affidavits sworn by a Mr Pinky Gay-trouser, 18, an unemployed youth of no fixed abode (though now living in Marbella thanks to the generosity of my clients).

Following an amicable out-of-court settlement, we have agreed to pay Mr John the sum of £1 million in appreciation of the very considerable damage to him and publicity to us.

For example, we have run a story in the *Sun* of to-day's date under the headline: "Sorry, Mate. No Hard Feelings! Geddit?!"

JUSTICE COCKLECARROT: This is disgraceful. The whole thing is a publicity stunt.

SIR EPHRAIM: Precisely, My Lord. We were hoping you'd say that because we have prepared a headline reading "Stuff It, Your Honour!" which will be printed on to-morrow's front page.

SIR HARTLEY REDFACE *(on behalf of Mr John):* My Lord, on behalf of my client I would like to express my thanks for the token sum of one million pounds and for the series of articles currently appearing in the *Sun* news-paper entitled: "Elton! Don'tcha Luv Him?", "20 Reasons Why Elton Is Brilliant", etc.

I would like to add that I shall be posing outside the court for photographs.

SIR EPHRAIM: So will I.

JUSTICE COCKLECARROT: So will I.

The case was concluded

I THINK I'M BEING FOLLOWED!

Duke of Hussey to attend Funeral of BBC

by Our Funeral Staff
William Randolph Hearse

It was today announced that Sir Marmalade Gussett, the self-styled "Duke of Hussey", will after all be attending the forthcoming State Funeral of the BBC.

In recent months, ever since it became clear that the BBC was "in its last days" and would shortly be succeeded by SKY-TV, there has been widespread speculation as to how Britain should react to the "end of an era".

For 60 years the BBC ruled the airwaves and was vested with an almost mystical authority.

Rising Sun

Many people in Britain felt that mourning was inappropriate and that the passing away of "Old Auntie" was "good riddance to bad rubbish".

But now the Duke of Hussey, who was personally present at the historic surrender of the BBC to the Government, has decided that it would be only fitting if he buried it himself.

How they are related

Almighty God

Ah So I (933-824 BC)	Apollo
Oh No (714-612)	King Stavros The Shifty of Macedonia
Princess Yoko	Alexander The Great
Emperor Datsun The Unreliable	Alexander The Hurricane *(Greek Snooker Champion 212-211 BC)*
Princess Nissan	Count Taki The Despicable — Princess Rudolfa of Hess
Dowager Empress Hiroshima	Baron von Reibnitz — Lord Louisa Von Mountbattenburg
The Mikado *(Produced by Dr Jonathan Miller. Seats available at all prices)*	HRH The Duke Of Edinburgh
Emperor Hirohitler of Japan	

"We couldn't afford a sprinkler system and a shower"

HAIKU CORNER

In Memoriam Emperor Hirohito

Ah so.
Farewell then
Emperor Hirohito.

E.J. Thribb (17½)

KENT
The Garden of England

For thousands of years the countryside of Kent has epitomised all that is best in England.

Sleepy oast houses. Apple blossom. Hops ripening in the late summer sun.

No wonder they call it the Garden of England. For garden it truly is.

But even the loveliest old garden can get boring after a bit. All that apple blossom, year after year. And the silence!

Doesn't anything ever happen here? you can imagine people saying.

And that's where British Rail comes into the picture.

For they've got plans to bring a bit of much-needed life into the old place.

To give the people of Kent something to talk about. Something to wake them up, even in the middle of the night.

Tired old Tonbridge. Sleepy Sevenoaks.

Tedious Tenterden. Drowsy Dartford. No longer!

They won't know what's hit them when our new 186 mph Paris-to-London non-stop Inter-City Super-Sizzlers come bulldozing through Kent on their way to the mystical East.

Just imagine the thrilling moment when those trains begin to thunder past, and even through, your very own lounge!

You will be able to look up from your arm-chair and see important celebrities like Lord Cockfield, Sir Leon Brittan and even Lord Suit himself hurtling past to vital business conferences in far-off exotic places like Limoges and Bruges. (There was a time when they had to "Fly to Bruges", as in the famous film. Remember?)

And you will have the satisfaction of knowing that you, the proud men of Kent, have once again — as so often before — been prepared to sacrifice everything for your country.

40 MINUTES TOO LONG
(BBC 2)

Scarfe's BEETHOVEN

(Opening shot of Gerald Scarfe playing Beethoven's Fifth on a kazoo whilst cycling around Bonn.)
SCARFE: Ever since I was a small boy I've loved Beethoven. He was a genius.

(Cut to Scarfe in Vienna painting huge protrait of himself.)
SCARFE: He's not the only genius though. It takes one to know one!
(Cut to Scarfe in Festival Hall wearing dinner jacket and holding baton.)
SCARFE: I've always fancied myself as a bit of a conductor.
(Cut to shot of Scarfe conducting huge orchestra paid for by BBC in front of audience of celebrities including Jane Asher and Gerald Scarfe.)
SCARFE: There's nothing to it really. It's just like drawing.

(Cut to arty animation showing baton turning into pen which produces caricatures of Beethoven admiring Scarfe's portrait of himself. Audience applaud wildly.)
SCARFE *(winking at camera)*: Life begins, after all, at piano forte.
(Cut to Scarfe dressed as Beethoven sitting at piano.)
SCARFE: Beethoven was born in 1770. I wasn't.
(Cut to picture of Scarfe as baby.)
SCARFE: I was born in 1936, exactly 166 years

"I won't have you cluttering up the room with your things!!"

later, yet I still enjoy his music as much as if I had written it myself.
(Shot of Max Miller in floral suit.)
MAX: There was this geezer, pal of mine, goes into the record shop and says, "My needle's worn out!" — no, not what you're thinking lady — so the girl behind the counter says: "Shall I feel your prick?" See?
(Cut to Scarfe.)
SCARFE *(to camera)*: Scarfe's the name lady, there'll never be another.
(Old archive film of Beethoven about to hang himself.)
BEETHOVEN: Zank Gott! Vun is too many!!

(Cut back to Scarfe dressed as Napoleon.)
SCARFE: Join me again next time when I look at myself through the eyes of Leonardo da Vinci, Van Gogh, William Blake, Gandhi . . .
(Music swells, Scarfe theme tune: "I'm in Love with a Wonderful Guy" by Gerry and the Documentary Makers. Credits roll.)

Presented by: Sir Gerald Scarfe
Script: Gerald Scarfe
(from an idea by G. Scarfe)
Rostrum camera: Gerry Scarfe
Key Grip: Geraldo Scarfe
Produced and Directed by Cecil B. De Scarfe

Prisoner of Conscience

No.94

Mrs Edwina Currie

In December 1988 Mrs Edwina Currie, who for some years had been one of the most outspoken and courageous political dissidents in Britain, suddenly disappeared after attacking the enormously powerful and mysterious Ministry of Egg and Fish.

Millions of Mrs Currie's sympathisers were shocked when she recently re-emerged, to make a partial recantation of her views to the all-powerful Select Committee on Eggri-culture. It was noticeable that Mrs Currie was not exhibited on the state media, but her recantation took the form of a "letter" to the Committee. Her supporters are convinced that the reason for this is that Mrs Currie must have been subjected behind the scenes to intensive "interrogation" to force her to "toe the party ine", and that she was not physically in a fit enough state to appear before the Committee in person.

They claim that it is "inconceivable" that Mrs Currie would ever have been prepared to admit that she was wrong unless "appalling pressure" had been applied to her.

Mrs Hatcher is 78.

St Cake's

Lonrho Term begins today. There are 16,002 boys in the school and one girl. Miss Pamella Bordes (Moynihan's) is Head Girl. B.S.B. Squarial (Fester's) is Master of the Dish. Perishing Worthless (Knight's) has been replaced as editor of the school magazine, *The Cakeian*, by Max Hastings (Hitler's). The Chaplain, Rev Julian Flowerbotham, has been replaced at short notice by the Mullah Ahmed Killrushdie, who becomes the school's first Director of Comparative Religions. The Barclaycard St Cake's Speech Day will be held on 21 June. Mr Adnan Khashoggi's place as Chief Speaker will be taken at short notice by Mr Ronnie Knight (O.C.). Performances of 'Allo, 'Allo will be given in the Maureen Lipman Technology and Craft Resource Centre on 21, 22, 23 June (tickets from the Bursar, General Alfredo Stroessner). The Trouser Game will be played on Chalfont's Meadow on 6 July. Exxons will be on 21 July. The O.C. Squash Fortnight will this year be held in the Ramada Hotel and Leisure Complex, Warrington (M79, junction 3). Bookings via the Secretary, Mr B.D. Airmiles (W.H.D. 1959-60).

THE SCANDAL OF THE CENTURY

Who are they — the principal players in the sex-shocker that is rocking the Government and has the nation gasping with boredom?

Hugo Dull, 43, the high-flying backbench MP for Legover, whom no one has ever heard of. He claims "never to have met" his former research assistant.

Pilau Rice-Davies — the so-called "research assistant" whose statistics proved vital!

Yves St Wyfront, 42, the mysterious French businessman she married for a night. Although he claims never to have met her, she has borne his cheque.

Simon Nobody, 35, the low-flying backbench MP for Trouserdown, who "never met" the woman he personally recommended for a security pass.

Lord Whitelaw, 87, former Deputy Leader of the Conservative Party. Claims "not to have a clue what is going on", and is probably right.

Mark Birk, 46, the sophisticated man-about-town editor of *Bedroom* magazine. Although he denies ever having met the winner of the Miss Poona Very Lovely Swimsuit 1979 contest, Jerk admits sleeping with her in the company of his wife.

Willy Jumper, 21, the brilliant National Hunt jockey. He said: "I have never met the former security risk, but she is the kind of woman I look up to."

Mustafa Hookah, 52. Feared boss of Col. Gaddafi's international terrorist organisation SEMTEX. He claims to have met Miss Rice-Davies on many occasions, in the hope of getting top Government secrets such as why the Tories are planning to privatise water.

Pick of the Movies
On Sky-TV Tonight

9.35 Black Pamuella Goes To Wapping. XXX.
Action starts when sultry former Miss India (Pamuella Strobes) takes off all her clothes in front of a rugged newspaper editor (Old Brill). It's wild, it's raunchy, it's deeply embarrassing. An erotic masterpiece firmly in the tradition of *Danish Dentist On The Job* and *Corfu, Wot A Bonker.*

Cast In Full

Brillo Pad . . .	Bruce Forsyth
Pamella	Mahadur
. . . .	Jaffrey Bernard
Man In Taxi	Colin
. . . .	Moynihan
Rupert Murdoch	Paul Hogan
Doald Trelford . .	John Hurt
Christine Keeler	Ian
. . . .	McKellen
Research Assistant	
. . . .	Samantha Fox

My naughty nights of love with hundreds of famous people

*By **Palmonella Borges**, as told to Glenda Lee-Potter*

MY LAST few weeks have been a living hell. I have been harried from continent to continent across the world by thousands of brutal, leering journalists intruding into my private life and offering me paltry sums to tell my life story.

I spurned them all, even though they fought tooth and nail to win me over.

But then, suddenly, one day I had a call from an old gentleman whose kind and generous cheque completely restored my faith in human nature. It was Lord Gnome.

That it why I have chosen *Private Eye* as the only organ caring and responsible enough to be a suitable vehicle for my story.

Chapter One: My Childhood *(Skip that. Ed.)*

Chapter Two: My Schooldays. *(Get on with the bonking. Ed.)*

Chapter Three: My Wild and Raunchy Nights with the Duke of Edinburgh. *(That's more like it. Ed.)* Unfortunately there weren't any.

Chapter Four: How Lord Denning Lured Me Into His Web of Evil.

When I first met the then Master of the Rolls I took him to be just a kindly old gentleman with a funny accent and an interest in the law.

But when I met him for a late-night "conference", I soon discovered that the only briefs he was interested in were mine! Geddit?!!

Chapter Five: The Bishop of Durham.

When I first met this saintly old theologian with his mitre and crook, I immediately knew that he was interested in me — and not just as a fellow atheist!

He had read all the sacred books of Islam, including the Kama Sutra — and he soon let me know his position with regard to this one!

Chapter Six: Sir Roy Strong.

I first met Sir Roy, as he liked to be called, when he was still the boss of Britain's sexiest museum, the V&A.

"Come up and see the Great Bed of Ware," he twinkled, with a come-hither flash of his famous moustache.

It was not an offer that a poor girl from India could refuse!

Chapter Seven: Sir Leonard Hutton.

The straightest bat I ever came across — if you know what I mean! — was that of the famous England cricketer Sir Leonard Hutton.

I often watched him on his tours of India when I was a small girl.

I once saw him score 409. Nearly as many as me — geddit?!?

Chapter Eight: Roy Plomley.

Many people think of the late Roy Plomley as just a voice on the radio asking people what they would like to have on a desert island.

The answer in his case was me!

(Note from Sue, Grabbit & Runne — Mr Plomley is deceased, so he can't sue. You can make up whatever you like.)

Chapter Nine: Ned Sherrin.

I first met the BBC's legendary Mr Twinky in the hospitality room of *Loose Ending*, the ever-popular radio comedy programme. But oddly enough I never got anywhere with him.

It has been literally a hell on earth to live through.

Here They Are – From Pamella's Own Album of Love – the men whom until now no one knew she had ever met..

Uncle Joe and Winnie — East meets West with little me in the middle!

Adolf — two in a bunker was his idea of fun!

My first love — Mahatma Gandhi.

A lot of people thought he was dead — but I knew better!

He had a dream — and I was it.

"Now look - you're doing it all wrong"

Lines Written To Commemorate The Historic Moment Of The Tenth Year And First Week In Power Of Our Beloved Prime Minister, Mrs Margaret Hilda Thatcher

It was in the month of May, nineteen hundred and
        eighty-nine
That the birds began to sing and the sun began to shine
And Whitehall was filled with cheering hordes
All hoping for a glimpse of the lovely Pamella Bordes.

Then suddenly out of the door of Number Ten
Stepped a vision of loveliness and her husband Den.
In her arms she cradled an infant bairn
Resembling a shellfish from the island of Pitcairn.

Also there in the radiant family group
Was her handsome son Mark, who had often been
        in the soup.
In many a Fleet Street tavern it was said
That his name had been linked with Mohammed Al-Fayed.

Nary a smile crossed his sullen face.
He looked like Lester Piggott after he had lost a race.
Nor was there a sign of the other twin —
No doubt writing a piece for the NatWest Cashcard
      holders' magazine called *Pin*.

And as her people gasped, she delivered a speech
In her familiar caring, high-pitched screech.
Quoting Kipling, she said: "I am a tigress."
Or was it Betjeman — but I digress.

They then adjourned to a sumptuous lunch
With the editors of all the newspapers except *Punch*.
Also there were famous men in suits from every walk of life.
Unfortunately there was no room for any of them to bring
        his wife.

So Maggie alone was the Queen of the May
In celebration of her momentous and very wonderful day.
And in tribute to the humble grocer's daughter from
        Grantham
They rose to their feet to sing the National Anthem.

They were then surprised to see coming in late
Another grocer, Mr Heath, whom she was supposed to hate.
'Twas thought she had invited him to this occasion
To prove that Britain was not a divided nation.

And so, after a day of laughter and tears,
People turned on to find yet another programme
        called *The Thatcher Years*.
And after weeks of being told that she was impossible
        to match
The whole nation decided that they were heartily sick
        of Thatch.

William McGonagall

PROFILE

Why Private Eye deserves to close

FEW tears will be shed by sensible people if, as a result of its present difficulties, Britain's most notorious weekly scandal sheet, *Private Eye*, is forced out of business.

A paper that shows such scant regard for the truth and deliberately prints so many casual inaccuracies and downright falsehoods does not deserve to survive.

Not a single issue goes by without its pages filled with irresponsible mistakes which, it is only too obvious, no one has bothered to check.

Since it was founded in 1953 by David Frost, Dr Jonathan Miller and Michael Foot, the paper has attracted its fair share of notoriety.

In 1964, for instance, it brought down the Macmillan government with its revelations about John Poulson and Jeremy Thorpe.

But then its leading investigative journalist Dudley Moore left for a new career in Hollywood and since then the magazine has sadly declined.

According to one insider: "Morale at the *Private*, as it is known to habitués of its weekly Monday lunches, has never been lower."

"On a recent occasion they invited Salman Rushdie to lunch and no one knew who he was. It's pathetic," says another insider (the same one).

Typical of the new style is the magazine's toadying attitude to people like Jeffrey Archer and Robert Maxwell, whom in the old days the *Eye* would have been the first to attack.

"This sort of thing would have been unthinkable when Nigel Dempster was the *Eye*'s News Editor in the 60s," says another Greek Street insider. "As a trained investigative journalist, Nigel would never have got his facts wrong like they do nowadays."

If *Private Eye* goes to the wall as a result of the current libel action by the wife of Denis Nilsson, its epitaph will fittingly be: "They never bothered to make that one phone call that could have made all the difference."

© *Worsthornetrash Productions, in co-operation with various sad men sacked from Private Eye ten years ago.*

If <u>that's</u> justice I'm a banana!

POETRY CORNER

In Memoriam Pressdram

So. Farewell
Then
Private Eye.

It serves
You right.

At least, that's
What Keith's
Mum says.

But then
She was on
The jury.

E.J. Thribb (£600,000)